PARISH LITURGIES

Experiments and Resources in Sunday Worship

by
Rev. Thomas Boyer

Editorial Assistant
Mary Sue Greer

PAULIST PRESS
New York / Paramus / Toronto

Library of Congress
Catalog Card Number: 73-81106

ISBN 0-8091-1776-2

Published by Paulist Press
Editorial Office: 1865 Broadway, N.Y., N.Y. 10023
Business Office: 400 Sette Drive, Paramus, N.J. 07652

Printed and bound in the
United States of America

CONTENTS

Contents

LITURGIES

To Bishop Victor J. Reed

"Pastors of souls must therefore realize that, when the liturgy is celebrated, something more is required than the mere observation of the laws governing valid and licit celebration; it is their duty also to ensure that the faithful take part fully aware of what they are doing, actively engaged in the rite and enriched by its effects" (Article 11, *Constitution on the Sacred Liturgy*).

That "something more is required" Bishop Reed was beautifully aware of. He realized that we are not merely urged to see beyond the law and yield to people's needs, but that we are required to do so, balancing both demands on the scale of the Church's mission in this world.

The newness of life and attitudinal shifts which Vatican Council II tried to stir, Bishop Reed allowed to stir in himself. In the area of liturgy alone, Bishop Reed seemed to exemplify what the developments are about: flexibility. He knew there was a definite structure to liturgy, but one of its nature, variable—to suit a particular people, a particular occasion. His concern was not variety for its own sake, but rather as a deeper expression of the "catholic" nature of the Church. As once was the case, external uniformity was no longer the discipline needed to lead people in prayer. Bishop Reed saw liturgy less as ritual and words, but more as an action of God's people in prayer, and God being glorified because these assembled people were made more fully alive through a prayer-experience in having communion with their Father.

Bishop Reed's work on the Bishop's Committee on the Liturgy, his interest and support of the Southwest Liturgical Conference, his attitude toward variety and flexibility in our own diocese, can best be honored it seems, by our own hard work in providing a variety in the forms of prayer with the assemblies we lead. The liturgy is the expression and formation of what it really means to be, to become, to beget the people of God; this demands that we be really CATHOLIC: in touch with the diversity of needs and people who form the Church of God.

   With warmth and affection then, this book is dedicated to Victor J. Reed—a man who wore well and who blessed us by not being easily intimidated by other men or by ideas differing from his own.

THE ORDER OF CELEBRATION

I. **The Entrance Rite**

    A. Invitation to Worship
    B. Processional
    C. Greeting
        Penitential Rite
            (within penitential seasons: Advent and Lent)
    D. Prayer of Invocation

II. **The Service of the Word**

    A. First Reading
    B. Response
    C. Second Reading
    D. Response and/or Gospel Acclamation
    E. The Gospel
    F. Gospel Acclamation
    G. Homily
    H. Profession of Faith
    I. General Intentions
    J. Period of Reflection: Intermission
    K. Processional
    L. Prayer of Blessing over Gifts

III. **The Table Prayer**

    A. Preface
    B. Hymn of Praise
    C. Acclamation directly following Consecration
    D. Acclamation elaborating "Amen" at conclusion of
        Eucharistic Prayer

IV. **The Service of Communion**

    A. The "Our Father"
    B. Rite of Peace

About these books

The volumes you are holding are a diary. They are much like the memories and experiences of a person recorded in privacy; not out of fear of discovery, but rather out of the suspicion that those things remembered and put away could be of interest to no one. At the time it seemed that the only purpose for the writing was to provide a measure with which to judge growth while recognizing and recovering from error.

Thus we have the beginnings of PARISH LITURGIES. These books should never be mistaken for some kind of recipe-books for the production of "instant liturgy." A glance ahead should make that very clear, for this is the diary of a community's life together; a community that exists to pray and to serve. It is a community that shares one thing with all others, the conviction that it is unique; that there is not another like it.

A closer look reveals that it is a group of youthful people. After all, the most avid diary keepers are usually the young. The three priests who served this parish during the time of this diary reflect the people themselves: two in their 20s and one in his 60s. It was the same in the pews: many young people and a sizable group of the old. If there is a generation gap, it was the missing middle age who are out in the suburbs. Part of the mystery at the Old Cathedral is that the young come, and the old stay with them. Together they are the Word Made Flesh, the Body of Christ.

In that setting, anonymity is preserved for those of tender years who are not yet able to risk identification. Yet there is also an *esprit de corps* among those who have come long enough and regularly enough to know one another by face and by name. Between the two there is respect and the kind of understanding that means support.

PREFACE

It is difficult to preface anything as incomplete as this work, but there will be no end to this effort as long as we remain a pilgrim Church. These liturgies are old now, and they look primitive alongside last week's; but then these are beginnings, the first stirrings of a renewed life in the risen Christ expressed through prayer.

A group gathered one night in the dining room of the rectory. They had been invited there because of a felt need—a need that called for more than one or two imaginations. They were people who could learn and who wanted to know more about their praying. They had said so from time to time. This group had also been invited because they had talents to share: they were secretaries who could type, artists who could visually express feelings and dreams, musicians who could lead the self-conscious, teachers with disciplined minds who could share ideas; and they were believers, all of them.

For several meetings they listened; then they questioned. They watched some liturgies being worked out by the priests. Always evaluating the past, they discussed the sermons: what could have been said, what was right and what was wrong. The questioning gave way to searching, and the watching gave way to pointing and directing; and in time they all worked together, asking: "Why?" "What for?" and "Why not?"

After some months, the group organized themselves as revolving teams—changing members to keep fresh, each team being assigned a date and a theme weeks ahead. They moved slowly, examining the past for its values and its mistakes, taking care to preserve the one while not repeating the other. Together they grew—sometimes in numbers, always in wisdom and understanding, certainly in grace.

As you go through this book, you will discover as our liturgy teams did that some incidentals come and go. "What's wrong with the Entrance Hymn?" someone asked. And someone else

answered that it took more than a few chords from the organ to
make him want to sing on most mornings. From this observation
grew the "Invitation" or "Call to Worship" which begins to appear
in later liturgies. It becomes, in time, a prayerful declaration of
just who we are and why we are together at the moment. From the
same discussion came the consensus that the Entrance Hymn was
more than a processional for the presiding minister. It was a
unifying experience; consequently, antiphonal music with cantor or
choir singing verses seemed inappropriate. We began to rely
most frequently on hymn-tunes.

Then the Entrance Rite came under consideration—its length
and the confusion the people experience over the sacramental
nature of absolution in that Rite. After much study in terms of
prayer effort and instruction of the people, it seemed appropriate to
emphasize the Penitential Rite during the Penitential seasons by
the addition of petitions in the form of a litany and, during the
Festive seasons, to occasionally omit the Penitential Rite, while
stressing the total aspect of reconciliation in another penitential
moment of the liturgy (e.g., the Greeting of Peace).

The Gospel, as the climactic point of the Service of the Word,
is always the center of attention. It is around this proclamation
that the entire structure of the liturgy unfolded for our planning
teams. This is one area where the gradual development is obvious
in these volumes: increasing emphasis is given the Gospel with
sung acclamations before and after. A somewhat dramatic pause
just before the proclamation, for the sake of reflection, also
developed as a way of underscoring the importance of the Gospel.

It was not at all uncommon for the liturgies to be turned in
with copious sermon notes attached by the team who had done the
preparation. In an effort to emphasize the true "offering" character
of the Anaphora prayer, the former "Offertory" came to be referred
to as the "Preparation Rite," the action completed directly and
often silently, letting the sign speak for itself. In time, the invocation
"Let us pray that my sacrifice and yours . . ." together with its
response became the only spoken transition from the Service of the
Word to the Table Prayer of Thanksgiving.

It seemed difficult for the congregation to move in spirit and
mood toward the priest's proclamation of the Table Prayer.

Consequently there evolved the practice of the faithful joining in with the Preface to deepen their sense of involvement and better prepare themselves to hear and appreciate the recalling of God's saving deeds in the Anaphora proper. Since all of the prefaces lead into song, the Great Prayer at the table is literally surrounded by song. A hymn of praise concludes each preface and also concludes the Prayer itself in the form of the "Doxology," which is called the "Ending Acclamation" in these volumes.

The liturgies in time developed a gentle sense of leisure; the silent periods reflect this best of all. A time of silence while the gifts are collected corresponds to a time of silence after they are returned. Communion over the word through the Homily is followed by reflection. Communion with the Body of Christ through signs of bread and wine is also followed by time for reflection upon the word and action preceding it. The prayer after Communion (the Prayer of Benediction) is a collect in the truest sense of the word, summarizing all that precedes it in word and action. As it flows right from the silent reflection which it concludes, the celebrant often remains seated as he leads this prayer. On occasion, song is a more fitting conclusion when particular lyrics summarize the total prayer of a celebration.

From such slow beginnings we have drawn these volumes. What worked three years ago in a downtown parish in the Middle West may work nowhere else this year. These volumes are offered for thought and study, that by reading and pondering we may deepen our understanding of what we do when we summon God's people together. May they never appear in a sanctuary, and may no people's identity be so denied that they be required to pray in these exact forms.

With deepest gratitude we remember:

Msgr. Raymond F. Harkin: There is no measure for his support, his wisdom, and his courage.

Rev. David Imming, Rev. William Saulnier, and Rev. Bill Skeehan: They continue to pour themselves out and are deeply loved.

Mary Sue Greer: She prays Father Gallen, Oosterhuis, and *Listen to Love* in her sleep. With this publication, may she begin to know some measure of peace.

And those beautiful ones who began: Geralda, Sis, Kathy, Sister Clotilda, Marie, John, Claudette, Joe, and Beverly.

FIRST SUNDAY OF ADVENT I

Theme: Time To Awake

THE ENTRANCE RITE

PROCESSIONAL:
"The Coming of Our God," *People's Mass Book,* #6.

GREETING:
Eucharistic Liturgies, p. 143.

PENITENTIAL RITE:
(*Response:* Lord, have mercy.)
For the times when we have chosen a way of darkness
    rather than light and truth, let us pray to the Lord:
For the times when we have chosen ignorance rather
    than honesty and awareness, let us pray to the Lord:
For the times when we have been silent out of fear,
    let us pray to the Lord:
For the times when we have resisted the movements of
    God's living spirit, let us pray to the Lord:

PRAYER OF INVOCATION:
Eucharistic Liturgies, p. 143.

THE SERVICE OF THE WORD

FIRST READING:
Isaiah 64:1–3(4).
(Reader lights the Paschal Candle.)

RESPONSE:
Ps. 80:1–2, 8–9, 14b–15, 17 (*by reader*). Ps. 80: 19a (*by people
—alternate with verses above*).

SECOND READING:
Romans 13:11–14.

1

RESPONSE:
"Send Forth Your Light and Your Truth" (Ps. 42, Antiphon II), *Twenty-Four Psalms and a Canticle*, p. 20.
(During this antiphon, the celebrant carries the Paschal Candle to the Advent Wreath and uses it to light the first candle.)

THE GOSPEL:
Mark 13:33–37.

HOMILY

PROFESSION OF FAITH

PERIOD OF REFLECTION:
Intermission

PROCESSIONAL:
"O Come, O Come, Emmanuel," *People's Mass Book*, #1.

PRAYER OF BLESSING OVER GIFTS:
Eucharistic Liturgies, p. 144.

THE TABLE PRAYER

PREFACE:
"Liturgy of the Lord of Light," *The Experimental Liturgy Book*, p. 109.

HYMN OF PRAISE:
"Holy, Holy, Holy," *People's Mass Book*, #106.

THE SERVICE OF COMMUNION

THE "OUR FATHER"

RITE OF PEACE

FRACTION RITE:
Litany of the "Lamb of God"

SONG:
> "Arise, Come to Your God" (Ps. 99, Antiphon II),
> *Twenty-Four Psalms and a Canticle*, p. 32.

PERIOD OF REFLECTION:
> Intermission

THE DISMISSAL RITE

PRAYER OF BENEDICTION:
> *Eucharistic Liturgies*, p. 144.

BLESSING AND DISMISSAL

ANNOUNCEMENTS

RECESSIONAL:
> "O God, Our Help in Ages Past," *People's Mass Book*, #185.

SECOND SUNDAY OF ADVENT I

Theme: Winter Is Waiting and Promise

THE ENTRANCE RITE

INVITATION TO WORSHIP:
Listen to Love, p. 14.

PROCESSIONAL:
"The Coming of Our God," *People's Mass Book*, #6.

GREETING:
Eucharistic Liturgies, p. 145.

PENITENTIAL RITE:
(*Response*: Lord, have mercy.)
Because of the times when we have given in to discouragement
during these times of waiting, we pray to the Lord:
Because of the times we have made idols of money, prestige,
and power while we await and anticipate the kingdom
that is already with us, we pray to the Lord:
Because we have been lazy, and have often chosen the
darkness of ignorance and prejudice rather than the
light of the truth which the Gospel offers us, we
pray to the Lord:

PRAYER OF INVOCATION:
Eucharistic Liturgies, p. 145.

THE SERVICE OF THE WORD

FIRST READING:
Isaiah 11:1-9.
RESPONSE:
Psalm 72:1-8, 17.

SECOND READING:
   2 Peter 3:8–13.

RESPONSE:
   Romans 8:22–25.

THE GOSPEL:
   Matthew 3:1–12. *(Luke 3:5–6 may be inserted between third and fourth verse as an elaboration.)*

GOSPEL ACCLAMATION:
   "O Lord, our God, you give your light, your word," *Your Word Is Near*, p. 20.
   (Celebrant lights two candles on Advent Wreath.)

HOMILY

GENERAL INTENTIONS:
   (*Response:* Lord, hear our prayer.)
   For those still standing in darkness, who have yet to
      hear God's Word of invitation because we have not
      spoken it by word or deed, let us pray to the Lord:
   For those poor and oppressed who are still awaiting
      the justice and freedom brought us already by Christ
      Jesus, whose Body we are, let us pray to the Lord:
   For those who teach and lead and serve, who become so
      tired and discouraged because we often fail to be
      responsive to their lessons, let us pray to the Lord:
   For those who are confused or harmed in any way by our
      double standards—those who are led to idols by our
      example during this time of waiting, let us pray to the Lord:

PERIOD OF REFLECTION:
   Intermission

PROCESSIONAL:
   "Maranatha," *People's Mass Book*, #8.

PRAYER OF BLESSING OVER GIFTS:
   Eucharistic Liturgies, p. 146.

THE TABLE PRAYER

PREFACE:
"The Canon of Christian Hope," *The Experimental Liturgy Book*, p. 71.

HYMN OF PRAISE:
"Holy, Holy, Holy," *People's Mass Book*, #106.

THE SERVICE OF COMMUNION

THE "OUR FATHER"

RITE OF PEACE

FRACTION RITE:
Litany of the "Lamb of God"

SONG:
"O Come, O Come, Emmanuel," *People's Mass Book*, #1.

PERIOD OF REFLECTION:
Intermission

THE DISMISSAL RITE

PRAYER OF BENEDICTION:
Eucharistic Liturgies, p. 146.

BLESSING AND DISMISSAL

ANNOUNCEMENTS

RECESSIONAL:
"Keep in Mind," *People's Mass Book*, #145.

THIRD SUNDAY OF ADVENT I

Theme: Joy in Waiting

THE ENTRANCE RITE

PROCESSIONAL:
"Let All the Earth Cry Out to the Lord" (Ps. 99), *People's Mass Book*, #156.

GREETING:
Eucharistic Liturgies, p. 149.

PENITENTIAL RITE:
(*Response:* Lord, have mercy.)
Because we have sometimes chosen to mourn with Christ
    rather than rejoice with him, we pray to the Lord:
Because we fail to overcome sadness with joy, the Joy
    of the Gospel message, we pray to the Lord:
Because we often choose a religion of the cross rather
    than a religion of an empty tomb, we pray to the Lord:
Because we sometimes fear—fear surprise which may give
    joy—and let that fear lead us to lives of suspicion
    and distrust, we pray to the Lord:

PRAYER OF INVOCATION:
Father, in the middle of this season of anticipation
    our joy begins to break out
    as we reflect on
    what your presence must mean for us.
As God you are so much better
    than any of us can imagine.
We expected a judge and avenger;
    you surprised us by presenting yourself as a child.
Make us receptive and open,
    and may we accept your kingdom
    as a child accepts bread
    from the hands of his Father.

7

Let us live in joy and peace
  at home with you
  all the days of our lives.
(Last two sentences adapted from "Make us receptive and
open," Huub Oosterhuis, *Your Word Is Near*, p. 19.)

THE SERVICE OF THE WORD

FIRST READING:
  Philippians 4:4–8.

RESPONSE:
  Paraphrase of "On Joy and Sorrow," *The Prophet*, pp. 28–29.

THE GOSPEL:
  John 16:20–22.

GOSPEL ACCLAMATION:
  Ps. 122:1–2, 8–9.
  (Celebrant lights three candles in Advent Wreath.)

HOMILY:
  If exceptionally good reader(s) is (are) available, pages
  169–173 of *A Tree Grows In Brooklyn* may be used in place
  of a homily. Cut appropriately.

GENERAL INTENTIONS:
  (*Response:* Lord, hear our prayer.)
  For those of us who, by our so-called adult understanding
    of the world, destroy the joy and hope of children,
    let us pray to the Lord:
  That we might come to understand that true joy exists
    in the concern and giving of one's self for the joy
    of another, let us pray to the Lord:
  By the joy-filled lives of Christian people, may the
    family of man experience once again the long-awaited
    and much-needed appearance of our Lord, let us pray
    to the Lord:

For the sick, the prisoners, the cold and hungry—for
the lonely, the outcast, the sinner—that they may
find cause for hope and joy because we care for them,
let us pray to the Lord:

PERIOD OF REFLECTION:
Intermission

PROCESSIONAL:
"The Coming of Our God," *People's Mass Book,* #6.

PRAYER OF BLESSING OVER GIFTS:
Eucharistic Liturgies, p. 148.

THE TABLE PRAYER

PREFACE:
"Canon of Joy," *The Experimental Liturgy Book,* p. 114.

HYMN OF PRAISE:
"Holy, Holy, Holy," *People's Mass Book,* #106.

THE SERVICE OF COMMUNION

THE "OUR FATHER"

RITE OF PEACE

FRACTION RITE:
Litany of the "Lamb of God"

SONG:
"Peace, My Friends," *Hymnal for Young Christians,* Vol. II,
p. 34.

PERIOD OF REFLECTION:
Intermission

THE DISMISSAL RITE

PRAYER OF BENEDICTION:
   Eucharistic Liturgies, p. 148.

BLESSING AND DISMISSAL

ANNOUNCEMENTS

RECESSIONAL:
   Same as Processional in Entrance Rite.

FOURTH SUNDAY OF ADVENT I

Theme: "The Sounds of Silence"
(This liturgy emphasizes the value of silence. The celebrant enters in silence and the reading below begins immediately.)

Reader: Genesis 1:26–27, 31a.

Celebrant: ". . . but then disorder came and man became less than he ought to be. He was driven from this place of openness and closeness with his God, and his relationships with others faltered at the same time."

Reponse: The reader reads the lyrics of Simon and Garfunkel's "I Am A Rock." The people join in on the lines, "I am a rock. I am an island." Lyrics may be found in *The Underground Mass Book*, p. 85.

Celebrant: ". . . but then came promises. All was not meant to remain in isolation. Man was called, invited from his room, his tomb. To us through Abraham he said . . ."

Reader: " 'I will be your God if you will be my people, and from you I shall raise up a nation of kings.' "

Celebrant: "From this invitation a certain people began the long business of restoring and rebuilding a relationship with God. These people, the sons of Abraham, communicated with God through the Prophets and in this way they learned many things about how their isolation was finally going to be ended once and for all . . ."

Reader: "The Prophet Isaiah said: 'Listen, House of David, the Lord himself will give you a sign. It is this: the maiden is with child and will soon give birth to her son whom she will call Immanuel' (Isaiah 7:14). The Prophet Micah said: 'Listen, sons of Abraham, out of you will be born for me the one who is to rule over Israel. He will stand and feed his flock with the power of Yahweh, with the majesty of the name of his God. They will live secure, for from then on he will extend his power to the ends of the land. He himself will be peace' (from Micah 5:2–4)."

Response: Hebrews 1:1–2 *(read by people)*.

Prayer: *Eucharistic Prayers,* p. 149.

Reader: "Realizing that we have been called back from our isolation and loneliness, we hear the words of the Prophet Isaiah." *(Here read Isaiah 35:1–7, 10.)*

Celebrant:
  Sign, Dec. 1969, p. 17, beginning with "Advent is a yearly reminder that the best of life is still ahead."

Reader: "Advent is waiting for something." *(Pause)*

Celebrant: "Advent is waiting for somebody." *(Pause)*

Reader: "Advent is waiting with somebody." *(Pause)*

Celebrant: "Advent is waiting for a new season." *(Pause)*

Reader: "Advent is waiting for a new life." *(Pause)*

Celebrant: "Advent is waiting for a new world." *(Pause)*
  (In silence the four candles of the Advent Wreath are lighted.)

THE GOSPEL:
  John 7:33–34. *(Add 20:22–23 if this liturgy is being used as penance service. In the latter case confessions would follow.)*

HOMILY

PERIOD OF REFLECTION:
  Intermission

PROCESSIONAL:
  "The Coming of Our God," *People's Mass Book,* #6.

PRAYER OF BLESSING OVER GIFTS:
  Eucharistic Liturgies, p. 150.

THE TABLE PRAYER

PREFACE:
  "Jesus Canon," first 16 lines, in *The Underground Mass Book,* p. 51.

HYMN OF PRAISE:
  "Holy, Holy, Holy," *People's Mass Book,* #106.

THE SERVICE OF COMMUNION

THE "OUR FATHER"

RITE OF PEACE

FRACTION RITE:
Litany of the "Lamb of God"

SONG:
"Peace, My Friends," *Hymnal for Young Christians*, Vol. II,
p. 34.

PERIOD OF REFLECTION:
Intermission

THE DISMISSAL RITE

PRAYER OF BENEDICTION:
Eucharistic Liturgies, p. 150.

BLESSING AND DISMISSAL

ANNOUNCEMENTS

RECESSIONAL:
"Joy To The World," *People's Mass Book*, #13.

FEAST OF IMMACULATE CONCEPTION I

Theme: Learning to Say "Yes"

THE ENTRANCE RITE

INVITATION TO WORSHIP:

> During this season of waiting, we pause to reflect on a person
> who really struggled in learning how to wait for light, for
> understanding, for faith. This person is Mary. Her greatness
> consists in having the faith to say "Yes" to God completely,
> to give thanks for what has been, and to say "Yes" or "Amen"
> to all that would come—even when it meant the cross. We
> gather to honor one of our own creation who is the pattern
> for our Christ-centered life and our giving birth to his presence
> in this century, on this day.

PROCESSIONAL:

> "Entrance Verse" (*spoken*), "A Marian Liturgy," *The
> Experimental Liturgy Book*, p. 160.

GREETING:

> Courage and strength, wisdom and blessings
>   be yours from God our Father,
>   who calls us
>   to total surrender to him in faith;
>   to complete happiness which comes
>   only through a life of selfless love.

PRAYER OF INVOCATION:

> Mindful of God's greatness in giving Mary to us,
>   let us pray:
> Father, faithful God, today we speak
>   our praises for your loving kindness.
> Our hearts rejoice that you as our Savior
>   have looked kindly upon your servant Mary.
> Because of the great things you did for her
>   and her own trust-filled confidence in you,

14

we can all regard ourselves as blessed.
We thank you for Mary,
   the pride of Israel, the boast of our race.
We praise you through her Son, Jesus,
   living within us forever and ever.

THE SERVICE OF THE WORD

FIRST READING:
   Proverbs 8:22–35.

RESPONSE:
   Luke 1:46–55.

SECOND READING:
   Thomas J. O'Connor in *Listen to Love*, p. 322.

RESPONSE:
   Silent reflection.

THE GOSPEL:
   Luke 1:26–38.

GOSPEL ACCLAMATION:
   Luke 1:42, 45.

HOMILY

PROFESSION OF FAITH

GENERAL INTENTIONS:
   (*Response:* Lord, hear our prayer.)
   That the Church, reflecting on Mary's faith, continue
      her search for the meaning of Christ in the modern
      world, we pray to the Lord:
   That the Church, in imitation of Mary's hope, realize
      that in her very weakness she will discover
      her fullness, we pray to the Lord:
   That the Church, contemplating Mary's love, be a

giver of life in response to the needs of men,
we pray to the Lord:

PERIOD OF REFLECTION:
Intermission

PROCESSIONAL:
"Of My Hands," *Hymnal for Young Christians*, p. 79.

PRAYER OF BLESSING OVER GIFTS:
Father, we are your people
gathered here to give you praise
for the new life you have offered to us
through Mary, your servant.
Receive the offering of our lives
which we place here in bread and wine
and join to the offering of your Son.
By these human signs of our love,
help us to grow in your service as did Mary
that your Son may be born anew in our midst
today and every day,
now and forever.
(Adapted from *Eucharistic Liturgies*, p. 150.)

THE TABLE PRAYER

PREFACE:
"Canon of Joy," *The Experimental Liturgy Book*, p. 114.

HYMN OF PRAISE:
"Holy, Holy, Holy," *People's Mass Book*, #106.

THE SERVICE OF COMMUNION

THE "OUR FATHER"

RITE OF PEACE

FRACTION RITE:
Litany of the "Lamb of God"

SONG:
"At That First Eucharist," *Our Parish Prays and Sings,* #11.

PERIOD OF REFLECTION:
Intermission

THE DISMISSAL RITE

PRAYER OF BENEDICTION:
Lord God, as with Mary, we do not know
    what will happen tomorrow or the day after.
This is not important.
What we do need and ask for now
    is trust and confidence in you,
    even though we may not always understand
    what you want of us.
Grant that we may live faith-filled lives
    with Jesus Christ, through whom we pray
    now and forever.

BLESSING AND DISMISSAL

ANNOUNCEMENTS

RECESSIONAL:
"Joy to the World," *People's Mass Book,* #13.

THE FEAST OF CHRISTMAS I
(Including the Solemn Closing of Advent)

Theme: Unto Us A Child Is Born

THE SERVICE OF THE WORD
The Solemn Closing of Advent

PROCESSION OF LIGHT:
> Lights in church are extinguished. Celebrant proceeds up main aisle with Paschal Candle from which the people's candles are lighted, row by row. All are singing "Come, O Lord, Oh, Come for Our Saving" (Is. 9:1–6, Antiphon II), *Biblical Hymns and Psalms*, p. 14.

FIRST READING:
> *(Reading is done by light of the Paschal Candle.)* Isaiah 9:1–6 (7). Begin with "The people that walked in darkness. . . ."

RESPONSE:
> "O Come, O Come, Emmanuel," *People's Mass Book*, #1.

SECOND READING:
> Micah 5:1 (2)—4a(5a).

RESPONSE:
> "O Little Town of Bethlehem" (*from any standard hymnal*).

THIRD READING
> Isaiah 11:1–9.

RESPONSE:
> "Silent Night," *People's Mass Book*, #12.

READING OF THE MARTYROLOGY:
> "The Liturgical Announcement of the Birth of Christ," ed. and prepared by Joseph T. Kush, C.G.M.

RESPONSE:
"The First Noel," *People's Mass Book*, #11. *(All lights are turned on.)*

PRAYER OF INVOCATION:
Eucharistic Liturgies, p. 151.

EPISTLE:
Titus 2:11–15.

GOSPEL ACCLAMATION:
"Unto Us A Child Is Born," *Biblical Hymns and Psalms*, p. 14.

THE GOSPEL:
Luke 2:1–20.

RESPONSE:
"O Come, All Ye Faithful," *People's Mass Book*, #9.

HOMILY

PROFESSION OF FAITH:
The Apostles' Creed

GENERAL INTENTIONS:
(*Response:* Lord, hear our prayer.)
That the spirit of Christmas, which is the spirit of Christian
joy and love, might not be set aside with the Christmas
tree, let us pray to the Lord:
That as we celebrate the event of God touching man we
would allow ourselves to be touched by him as he comes
to us today in the poor, the sick, the lonely, the oppressed,
let us pray to the Lord:
For all people of all ages, for all who, young and old, belong
to each other and go through life together, let us pray to
the Lord:
For all the people of this parish, for all here this evening,
for the people of (city)—that we may be aware of our God
who has pitched his tent among us, let us pray to the Lord:

PRAYER:

> Lord our God, we celebrate this night the birth of Jesus,
> your Son our Lord, light of the world. We ask you to let
> us see in him your grace and goodness; we ask that his light
> may shine forth now and always. Lord God and Father of
> Jesus Christ, this is the night when he was born, our hope
> and our salvation. Let his light shine in our lives; may we love
> him and keep him—your Word among us, your peace on
> earth, today and every day, world without end.

PERIOD OF REFLECTION:

> Intermission

PROCESSIONAL:

> "Angels We Have Heard on High," *People's Mass Book,* #16.

PRAYER OF BLESSING OVER GIFTS:

> *Eucharistic Liturgies,* p. 152.

THE TABLE PRAYER

PREFACE:

> "Liturgy of the Lord of Light," *The Experimental Liturgy
> Book,* p. 109.

HYMN OF PRAISE:

> "Holy, Holy, Holy! Lord God Almighty," *People's Mass Book,*
> #184.

THE SERVICE OF COMMUNION

THE "OUR FATHER"

RITE OF PEACE

FRACTION RITE:

> Litany of the "Lamb of God"

SONG:
"Peace My Friends," *Hymnal for Young Christians*, Vol. II,
p. 34.

PERIOD OF REFLECTION:
Intermission

THE DISMISSAL RITE

PRAYER OF BENEDICTION:
Eucharistic Liturgies, p. 152.

BLESSING AND DISMISSAL

ANNOUNCEMENTS

RECESSIONAL:
"Joy to the World," *People's Mass Book*, #13.

SUNDAY WITHIN THE OCTAVE OF CHRISTMAS I

Theme: "Joy to the World"

THE ENTRANCE RITE

PROCESSIONAL:
"Angels We Have Heard On High," *People's Mass Book*, #6.

GREETING:
Eucharistic Liturgies, p. 154.

PRAYER OF INVOCATION:
Eucharistic Liturgies, p. 154.

THE SERVICE OF THE WORD

FIRST READING:
Isaiah 41:8–16.

RESPONSE:
Isaiah 42:1–4.

SECOND READING:
Galatians 4:1–7.

GOSPEL ACCLAMATION:
"Unto Us A Child Is Born," *Biblical Hymns and Psalms*, p. 14.

THE GOSPEL:
Luke 2:33–40.

RESPONSE:
Luke 2:29–32.

HOMILY

PERIOD OF REFLECTION:
Intermission

PROCESSIONAL:
"O Come, All Ye Faithful," *People's Mass Book*, #9.

PRAYER OF BLESSING OVER GIFTS:
Eucharistic Liturgies, p. 155.

THE TABLE PRAYER

PREFACE:
"Canon of Joy," *The Experimental Liturgy Book,* p. 114.

HYMN OF PRAISE:
"Holy, Holy, Holy," *People's Mass Book,* #106.

THE SERVICE OF COMMUNION

THE "OUR FATHER"

RITE OF PEACE

FRACTION RITE:
Litany of the "Lamb of God"

SONG:
"Priestly People," *People's Mass Book,* #146.

PERIOD OF REFLECTION:
Intermission

THE DISMISSAL RITE

PRAYER OF BENEDICTION:
Eucharistic Liturgies, p. 155.

BLESSING AND DISMISSAL

ANNOUNCEMENTS

RECESSIONAL:
"O Come, All Ye Faithful," *People's Mass Book,* #9.

NEW YEAR'S CELEBRATION OF PEACE I

Theme: Peace

THE ENTRANCE RITE

PROCESSIONAL:
"Peace, My Friends," *Hymnal for Young Christians*, Vol. II, p. 34.

GREETING:
The priest says the first line of the "Glory to God." People join for remainder.

PRAYER OF INVOCATION:
Father, you have told us
   that peacemakers shall be called
   your favorite sons.
Help us, then, to work tirelessly
   and more enthusiastically
   for that justice which alone
   can bring true and lasting peace.
Through Jesus, your Son,
   who with you and the Spirit
   lives as God forever.

THE SERVICE OF THE WORD

FIRST READING:
Isaiah 2:2–5.

RESPONSE:
"Invitation to Worship," *Interrobang*, pp. 76–77.

SECOND READING:
James 3:14–18.

GOSPEL ACCLAMATION:
"All the Earth Proclaim the Lord," *Biblical Hymns and Psalms*, p. 72.

THE GOSPEL:
    Matthew 5:38–48.

GOSPEL ACCLAMATION:
    Repeat from above.

HOMILY

GENERAL INTENTIONS:
    Selection from pp. 125–126, Huub Oosterhuis, *Your Word Is Near.*

PERIOD OF REFLECTION:
    Intermission

PROCESSIONAL:
    "Praise God From Whom All Blessings Flow," *People's Mass Book,* #45.

PRAYER OF BLESSING OVER GIFTS:
    Father, these gifts are symbols
        of peace and unity.
    Through the sacrifice-gift of your Son,
        the king of peace,
        may they strengthen the bonds
        of harmony and good will among men.
    Through Jesus Christ, your Son,
        who with you and the Spirit
        lives as God forever.

THE TABLE PRAYER

PREFACE:
    "Eucharistic Prayer of Human Unity," *The Experimental Liturgy Book,* p. 100.

HYMN OF PRAISE:
    "Holy, Holy Holy! Lord God Almighty," *People's Mass Book,* #184.

ACCLAMATION AT CONSECRATION:
"Keep in Mind," *People's Mass Book*, #145.

THE SERVICE OF COMMUNION

THE "OUR FATHER"

RITE OF PEACE

FRACTION RITE:
Litany of the "Lamb of God"

SONG:
"My Shepherd Is the Lord" (Ps. 22, Antiphon I), *Twenty-Four Psalms and a Canticle*, p. 10.

PERIOD OF REFLECTION:
Intermission

THE DISMISSAL RITE

PRAYER OF BENEDICTION:
Lord and God, we pray that you may give us
    the spirit of love.
May we, who are nourished
    by the body and blood of your only Son,
    foster among people that peace
    which he gave us.
Through Jesus Christ, your Son,
    who with you and the Spirit,
    lives as God forever.

BLESSING AND DISMISSAL

ANNOUNCEMENTS

RECESSIONAL:
"Rejoice, the Lord Is King," *Hymnal for Young Christians*, p. 115.

EPIPHANY SUNDAY I

Theme: "Your Light Has Come"

THE ENTRANCE RITE

PROCESSIONAL:
"The First Noel," *People's Mass Book,* #11.

GREETING:
Eucharistic Liturgies, p. 162.

PRAYER OF INVOCATION:
Eucharistic Liturgies, p. 162.

THE SERVICE OF THE WORD

FIRST READING:
Isaiah 60:1–6.

RESPONSE:
Rosemary Haughton in *Listen to Love,* p. 256.

SECOND READING:
The lyrics of "Aquarius," James Rado and Gerome Ragni.
This should be introduced with a brief explanation of the
signs of the zodiac and the suggestion that the lyrics of
"Aquarius" relate to Sacred Scripture and the dream all of us
share because of our light, Jesus Christ.

RESPONSE:
Silent reflection.

THE GOSPEL:
Matthew 2:1–12.

RESPONSE:
"A Christmas Carol," *Your Word Is Near,* p. 46.

HOMILY

GENERAL INTENTIONS:
(*Response:* Lord, make us a light for all to see.)
For those who are saddened and discouraged by their
difficulties in life, that they might find strength in our
sharing of their burdens, we pray to the Lord:
For those who seek understanding and support as they
search to find their way in life, we pray to the Lord:
For our world, as it enters a new decade, that it may
find a guiding star in the Church, we pray to the Lord:
For our parish family, that among us harmony and
understanding, sympathy and trust may be abounding, we
pray to the Lord:

PERIOD OF REFLECTION:
Intermission

PROCESSIONAL:
"Send Forth Your Light" (Ps. 42, Antiphon II), *Twenty-Four
Psalms and a Canticle,* p. 20.

PRAYER OF BLESSING OVER GIFTS:
Eucharistic Liturgies, p. 160.

THE TABLE PRAYER

PREFACE:
"Liturgy of the Lord of Light," *The Experimental Liturgy
Book,* p. 109.

HYMN OF PRAISE:
"Holy, Holy, Holy," *People's Mass Book,* #106.

ACCLAMATION AT CONSECRATION:
"Keep in Mind," *People's Mass Book,* #145.

THE SERVICE OF COMMUNION

THE "OUR FATHER"

RITE OF PEACE

FRACTION RITE:
   Litany of the "Lamb of God"

SONG:
   "Sion, Sing," *People's Mass Book,* #165.

PERIOD OF REFLECTION:
   Intermission

THE DISMISSAL RITE

PRAYER OF BENEDICTION:
   Eucharistic Liturgies, p. 161.

BLESSING AND DISMISSAL

ANNOUNCEMENTS

RECESSIONAL:
   "The First Noel," *People's Mass Book,* #11.

FIRST SUNDAY AFTER EPIPHANY I

Theme: The Baptism of Our Lord

THE ENTRANCE RITE

INVITATION TO WORSHIP:
Luke 2:41–52.

PROCESSIONAL:
"Sion, Sing," *People's Mass Book*, #165.

GREETING:
Eucharistic Liturgies, p. 163.

PRAYER OF INVOCATION:
"Lord God, we speak with reverence," *Your Word Is Near*,
p. 57.

THE SERVICE OF THE WORD

FIRST READING:
Philippians 2:5–11.

RESPONSE:
Rod McKuen in *Listen to Love*, p. 246.

SECOND READING:
Hans Küng in *Listen to Love*, p. 160.

GOSPEL ACCLAMATION:
"Glory to God, Glory," *Hymnal for Young Christians*, p. 71.

THE GOSPEL:
John 1:29–34.

GOSPEL ACCLAMATION:
Repeat from above.

HOMILY

GENERAL INTENTIONS:
(*Response:* Son of God, hear our prayer.)

That in these times of great change and uncertainty over things to come, the Christian people by their faith and hope would offer a spirit of optimism and confidence to a world of men seeking meaning in life, we pray to the Lord:

For all Christians, joined together in the one Christ by the waters of baptism, that we may continue in our understanding of one another, and work together to offer the world a Christian viewpoint on all life's situations, we pray to the Lord:

For ourselves, that we may have the courage and determination to live the Christian life in such a manner that those about us would experience the value and meaning of Jesus in their lives, we pray to the Lord:

For the sick and the lonely, for those in sorrow, for the leaders of our country and of the Church, for those members of our family who have died—for all these, we ask God's peace, we pray to the Lord:

PERIOD OF REFLECTION:
Intermission

PROCESSIONAL:
"We Gather Together," *People's Mass Book,* #53.

PRAYER OF BLESSING OVER GIFTS:
Eucharistic Liturgies, p. 164.

THE TABLE PRAYER

PREFACE:
"The Canon of Christian Hope," *The Experimental Liturgy Book,* p. 71.

HYMN OF PRAISE:
"Praise to the Lord," *People's Mass Book,* #175.

ACCLAMATION AT CONSECRATION:
    "Keep in Mind," *People's Mass Book*, #145.

THE SERVICE OF COMMUNION

THE "OUR FATHER"

RITE OF PEACE

FRACTION RITE:
    Litany of the "Lamb of God"

SONG:
    "At the Lamb's High Feast," *Our Parish Prays and Sings*, #2.

PERIOD OF REFLECTION:
    Intermission

THE DISMISSAL RITE

PRAYER OF BENEDICTION:
    Eucharistic Liturgies, p. 164.

BLESSING AND DISMISSAL

ANNOUNCEMENTS

RECESSIONAL:
    "All Glory, Praise and Honor," *People's Mass Book*, #29.

SECOND SUNDAY AFTER EPIPHANY I

Theme: The Marriage Feast of Cana

THE ENTRANCE RITE

INVITATION TO WORSHIP

Reader: Today, Cana Sunday, we celebrate God's Covenant with man as it is made manifest by the sign of marriage. The relationship between God and man, Christ and his Church, is no less real and a part of our lives today than is the living relationship between husband and wife. St. Paul invites us to give way to one another in service to Christ. A man should love a woman . . .

Men: Just as Christ loved the Church and sacrificed himself for her to make her holy.

Reader: Give way to one another in service to Christ. A woman should love a man . . .

Women: Just as the Church loves Christ and offers herself to him so that his love can continue to be made known.

Reader: Christ made the Church clean by washing her in water with a form of words; so that when he took her to himself she would be glorious, holy and faultless. In the same way, husbands must love their wives as they love their own bodies:

Men: For a man to love his wife is for him to love himself.

Reader: In the same way, wives must love their husbands as they love their own bodies:

Women: A woman never hates her own body but she feeds it and looks after it: so she must do the same for her loved one.

Reader: For the two have become one. And that is the way Christ treats the Church because it is his body and we are his living parts.

(An adaptation of Ephesians 5:21–33.)

PROCESSIONAL:
"We Gather Together," *People's Mass Book*, #53.

GREETING:
Eucharistic Liturgies, p. 165.

PRAYER OF INVOCATION:
   Eucharistic Liturgies, p. 165. Omit second and fifth sentences.

THE SERVICE OF THE WORD

FIRST READING:
   Isaiah 54:7–10 or 62:1–4.

RESPONSE:
   Ephesians 4:15–16.

SECOND READING:
   Romans 12:6–16.

GOSPEL ACCLAMATION:
   "Glory to God, Glory," *Hymnal for Young Christians,* p. 71.

THE GOSPEL:
   John 2:1–12.

RESPONSE:
   Dag Hammarskjold in *The Underground Mass Book,* p. 57;
   or Robert Penn Warren in *Horizons of Hope,* p. 64.

GOSPEL ACCLAMATION:
   Repeat from above.

HOMILY

PROFESSION OF FAITH, WEDDING CREED, AND VOWS:
   "A Wedding Liturgy," *The Experimental Liturgy Book,* p. 143.

GENERAL INTENTIONS:
   (*Response:* Lord, hear our prayer.)
   That all Christians remember that they were made one in
      Christ through holy baptism, we pray to the Lord:
   That all Christians be mindful that our oneness in Christ is
      strengthened by the Holy Eucharist, we pray to the Lord:
   That all Christians, all men and women, use their unique

talents and capabilities in the service of all those who call
upon them, we pray to the Lord:

That all married Christians would be mindful that they are
living signs of the union of the Church with our Father in
heaven, we pray to the Lord:

PERIOD OF REFLECTION:
Intermission

PROCESSIONAL:
"Rejoice, the Lord Is King," *Hymnal for Young Christians,*
p. 115.

PRAYER OF BLESSING OVER GIFTS:
Eucharistic Liturgies, p. 166.

THE TABLE PRAYER

PREFACE:
Preface (3), "The Rite for Celebrating Marriage during Mass,"
Manual of Celebration, p. 15.

HYMN OF PRAISE:
"Praise to the Lord," *People's Mass Book,* #175.

ACCLAMATION AT CONSECRATION:
"Keep in Mind," *People's Mass Book,* #145.

THE SERVICE OF COMMUNION

THE "OUR FATHER"

RITE OF PEACE

FRACTION RITE:
Litany of the "Lamb of God"

SONG:
"My Shepherd Is the Lord" (Ps. 22, Antiphon I), *Twenty-Four
Psalms and a Canticle,* p. 10.

PERIOD OF REFLECTION:
   Intermission

THE DISMISSAL RITE

CONCLUDING PRAYER AND BLESSING:
   "The Rite for Celebrating Marriage during Mass," *Manual of Celebration*, p. 20.

ANNOUNCEMENTS

RECESSIONAL:
   "All Glory, Praise, and Honor," *People's Mass Book*, #29.

THIRD SUNDAY AFTER EPIPHANY I

Theme: God's Presence Among Men

THE ENTRANCE RITE

INVITATION TO WORSHIP:
Ritual and Life, Preface, beginning with "Ritual and life are bound together . . ." and ending with "Life lived in awareness." Continue with p. 59 beginning with "Life is in us . . ." and ending with "This is the Christian belief." People respond with p. 59, beginning with "The Christian life is an acting out . . ." and ending with ". . . its promise will be kept."

PROCESSIONAL:
"We Gather Together," *People's Mass Book,* #53.

GREETING:
Eucharistic Liturgies, p. 175.

PRAYER OF INVOCATION:
Eucharistic Liturgies, p. 175. May be abbreviated by omitting third and fifth sentences.

THE SERVICE OF THE WORD

FIRST READING:
Leviticus 13:1–2, 45–46.

RESPONSE:
Ritual and Life, p. 59, beginning with "Sometimes when a game . . ." and ending with ". . . inertia and isolation are overcome."

SECOND READING:
1 Corinthians 11:23–26.

GOSPEL ACCLAMATION:
"Alleluia!, Alleluia!," *Biblical Hymns and Psalms,* Vol. II, p. 88.

THE GOSPEL:
   Mark 1:40–45.

GOSPEL ACCLAMATION:
   Repeat from above.

HOMILY

GENERAL INTENTIONS:
   (*Response:* O Lord, hear our prayer.)
   For all Christian people, that we might realize we are to be
      a sign of God's presence in this world by all that we say
      and do, let us pray to the Lord:
   For ourselves, that we may never allow those about us to
      become victims of our misunderstanding or misjudgment,
      let us pray to the Lord:
   For all Christian people, that everything we do may be done
      as a continual act of praise to God, our Father, let us pray
      to the Lord:

PERIOD OF REFLECTION:
   Intermission

PROCESSIONAL:
   "Rise Up, O Men Of God," *The Hymnal of the Protestant
   Episcopal Church in the United States of America*, #535.

PRAYER OF BLESSING OVER GIFTS:
   Eucharistic Liturgies, p. 176, first three sentences. Add:
   All of this we do in the name of Jesus,
   who with you and the Holy Spirit,
   lives as God, forever and ever.

THE TABLE PRAYER

PREFACE:
   "Eucharistic Prayer by John C. L'Heureux," *The Experimental
   Liturgy Book*, p. 97. May be abbreviated by omitting lines
   12–15.

HYMN OF PRAISE:
   "Praise God, From Whom All Blessings Flow," *People's Mass Book,* #45.

ACCLAMATION AT CONSECRATION:
   "Keep in Mind," *People's Mass Book,* #145.

ENDING ACCLAMATION:
   #108b, *People's Mass Book.*

THE SERVICE OF COMMUNION

THE "OUR FATHER"

RITE OF PEACE

FRACTION RITE:
   Litany of the "Lamb of God"

SONG:
   "O Taste and See the Goodness of the Lord," *Psalms for Singing,* Book One, p. 14.

PERIOD OF REFLECTION:
   Intermission

THE DISMISSAL RITE

PRAYER OF BENEDICTION:
   Eucharistic Liturgies, p. 176.

BLESSING AND DISMISSAL

ANNOUNCEMENTS

RECESSIONAL:
   "Now Thank We All Our God," *People's Mass Book,* #178.

FOURTH SUNDAY AFTER EPIPHANY I
(or Sunday nearest February 2)

Theme: The Festival of Light

THE ENTRANCE RITE

INVITATION TO WORSHIP:
    Matthew 5:14–16.

PROCESSIONAL:
    "Sion, Sing," *People's Mass Book*, #165.

GREETING:
    Eucharistic Liturgies, p. 160.

PRAYER OF INVOCATION:
    Grateful for the light of Christ which has touched our lives,
        let us pray:
    Father, we your people rise up in splendor, for your light
        has come; the glory of you, our God, shines now upon us.
    We are grateful for this light, who is Jesus Christ, your Son,
        who brightens our lives and guides us along the only path
        to you.
    Open our eyes that we may see the light that comforts us,
        the kindly light, and hear your good news for this world
        for ever and ever.
    (Adapted from *Eucharistic Liturgies*, p. 160.)

THE SERVICE OF THE WORD

FIRST READING:
    Malachi 3:1–4.

RESPONSE:
    Rosemary Haughton in *Listen to Love*, p. 256.

THE GOSPEL:
    Luke 2:22–32.

THE BLESSING OF THE CANDLES:

For light to recognize God's saving presence which transforms us and always makes us new in Christ, let us pray: (*pause*) Holy Father, almighty and eternal God, on this day on which you granted the just man Simeon his request, we ask you to bless, + to sanctify, + and to kindle these candles with the light of your heavenly blessing. A visible flame lights these candles to dispel the darkness of night; and so we ask your spirit to enlighten our hearts and free us from all blindness of sin. From your place of glory, hear the voices of your people taking these candles and carrying them lighted, offering you honor and praise with song.
(Adapted from "Prayers for Blessing of Candles," in *The English-Latin Sacramentary.*)

THE PROCESSION:

Celebrant intones the "Glory be to God" and begins procession, sharing his light with the congregation who received candles upon entering the church. If this hymn finishes before the procession has returned to sanctuary, sing "Bless the Lord," *Hymnal for Young Christians*, p. 71.

PROFESSION OF FAITH:

Still holding lighted candles, all read together John 1:1–5, 9–12a, 16–18. Then all candles are extinguished.

HOMILY

GENERAL INTENTIONS:

(*Response:* Lord, make us a light for all to see.)

That the brilliance of Christ's presence may never be dimmed by further disunity, distrust, and alienation, let us pray to the Lord:

That the light of Christ may assist us to see ourselves as others see us, let us pray to the Lord:

For the light of wisdom and courage within our diocesan council and with our own four delegates as they meet in deanery assembly this coming week, let us pray to the Lord:

(Congregation using this liturgy may adapt this petition to fit a particular need of the parish.)

For the courage never to choose the darkness of ignorance when it seems to be an easy escape from the problems which oppress us, let us pray to the Lord:

PRAYER:

Father of Jesus Christ, our God, confirm and strengthen our belief that it is he whom we expect and that your light has shone in him upon the world. We pray to you, take from us everything that cannot bear this light and make us love your peace.

PERIOD OF REFLECTION:

Intermission

PROCESSIONAL:

"Rejoice, the Lord Is King," *Hymnal for Young Christians,* p. 115.

PRAYER OF BLESSING OVER GIFTS:

Father, may these gifts be transformed into living signs of your presence, so that we who seek oneness through your Son's body and blood may become light for those who are in darkness.

We ask this through Jesus your Son who illumines our lives with hope, living and reigning with the Holy Spirit, forever and ever.

THE TABLE PRAYER

PREFACE:

"Liturgy of the Lord of Light," *The Experimental Liturgy Book,* p. 109.

HYMN OF PRAISE:

"Holy, Holy, Holy! Lord God Almighty," *People's Mass Book,* #184.

ACCLAMATION AT CONSECRATION:
   "Keep in Mind," *People's Mass Book*, #145.

THE SERVICE OF COMMUNION

THE "OUR FATHER"

RITE OF PEACE

FRACTION RITE:
   Litany of the "Lamb of God"

SONG:
   "At the Lamb's High Feast," *Our Parish Prays and Sings*, #2.

PERIOD OF REFLECTION:
   Intermission

THE DISMISSAL RITE

PRAYER OF BENEDICTION:
   With faith and with love, Father, we have renewed our
   awareness of your life-giving presence.
   Remembering the blessed St. Blaise, who by his faith in your
   promises was worthy of your blessings, we ask that all of
   us standing in your presence might share in the same
   health and happiness; that by our voices we might make
   known your glory day by day.

BLESSING AND DISMISSAL

ANNOUNCEMENTS

RECESSIONAL:
   "Holy God, We Praise Thy Name," *People's Mass Book*, #176.

FIFTH SUNDAY AFTER EPIPHANY I
(Appropriate for Parish, Deanery, and Diocesan Meetings)

Theme: Intra-Church Dialogue

THE ENTRANCE RITE

INVITATION TO WORSHIP:
   The celebrant should set the theme for the liturgy in terms
   of the particular occasion.

PROCESSIONAL:
   "Priestly People," *People's Mass Book*, #146.

GREETING:
   Eucharistic Liturgies, p. 16.

PRAYER OF INVOCATION:
   Eucharistic Liturgies, p. 172.

THE SERVICE OF THE WORD

FIRST READING:
   1 Corinthians 13:1–13.

RESPONSE:
   "Eight Ground Rules for Intra-Church Dialogue," *Critic*, Vol.
   28, Nov.–Dec. 1969, pp. 92–93. This response is followed by
   a short time for reflection.

GOSPEL ACCLAMATION:
   "Glory to God, Glory," *Hymnal for Young Christians*, p. 71.

THE GOSPEL:
   Luke 18:3–43.

RESPONSE:
   Colossians 3:12–15. Change "you," "your," or "yours" to "we,"
   "us," "our," or "ours."

HOMILY

GENERAL INTENTIONS:
> (*Response:* Son of David, have pity on us and let us see
> again.)
> That in the painful process of coming to a realization of
> who we are as Christians and what we are about, we would
> have a true sense of hope and faith in Christ present with
> us, we pray to the Lord:
> That the people of ———— would respond to their task of
> renewing the Church so that we might be a continuing sign
> of Christ in our community, we pray to the Lord:
> For the many times when we have failed as individuals and
> as a community to be understanding and accepting of others
> —that we may have the courage to change what there is in
> us that is not of Christ, we pray to the Lord:

PERIOD OF REFLECTION:
> Intermission

PROCESSIONAL:
> "Praise the Lord, O Heavens," *People's Mass Book*, #181.

PRAYER OF BLESSING OVER GIFTS:
> *Eucharistic Liturgies*, p. 17.

THE TABLE PRAYER

PREFACE:
> "The Canon of the Pilgrim Church," *The Experimental Liturgy
> Book*, p. 73.

HYMN OF PRAISE:
> "Praise God, From Whom All Blessings Flow," *People's Mass
> Book*, #45.

ACCLAMATION AT CONSECRATION:
> "Keep in Mind," *People's Mass Book*, #145.

THE SERVICE OF COMMUNION

THE "OUR FATHER"

RITE OF PEACE

FRACTION RITE:
Litany of the "Lamb of God"

SONG:
"They'll Know We Are Christians by Our Love," *Hymnal for Young Christians*, p. 132.

PERIOD OF REFLECTION:
Intermission

THE DISMISSAL RITE

PRAYER OF BENEDICTION:
Eucharistic Liturgies, p. 17.

BLESSING AND DISMISSAL

ANNOUNCEMENTS

RECESSIONAL:
"Rejoice, the Lord is King," *Hymnal for Young Christians*, p. 115.

ASH WEDNESDAY I
The Solemn Opening of Lent

Theme: "To Dust You Shall Return"

THE ENTRANCE RITE

INVITATION TO WORSHIP:
Genesis 2:5–7, 18–22; 3:17a–19. Preface lines from third
chapter with "Addressing man after their sin, Yahweh said
to them, 'Accursed. . . .'"

PROCESSION:
The reader lights the fire; the ministers are carrying palms
which, upon their arrival at the fire, are put into the fire.
The people are singing "Have Mercy On Me" (Ps. 50,
Antiphon I), *Twenty-Four Psalms and a Canticle*, p. 22.

GREETING AND PRAYER OF INVOCATION:
Eucharistic Liturgies, p. 18.

THE SERVICE OF THE WORD

FIRST READING:
Joel 2:12–19.

RESPONSE:
"Yes, I Shall Arise," *People's Mass Book*, #174.

THE GOSPEL:
Matthew 6:16–21.

RESPONSE:
Blessing of the Ashes. Use *The English-Latin Sacramentary*
prayer of blessing of the ashes, beginning, "You desire not
the death but the repentance of sinners." Preface with:
"Let us pray to God to have pity as we humbly accept this
sign of penance."

PROCESSION:
> During distribution of ashes, the following prayer is led by a
> deacon or server and responded to by the people: "Service
> of Penance and Ashes," *Eucharistic Liturgies*, p. 19 up to
> "Father of mercy and Father of Love. . . ." This last prayer
> is said by the people as the minister is washing his hands
> after the distribution. Then the minister prays the absolutions
> given in the same source, p. 20. All are invited to gather
> around the altar after receiving ashes. The bread and wine
> are brought forward.

PRAYER OF BLESSING OVER GIFTS:
> *Eucharistic Liturgies*, p. 21.

THE TABLE PRAYER

PREFACE:
> Preface for Lent in *The English-Latin Sacramentary*.

HYMN OF PRAISE:
> "Holy, Holy, Holy! Lord God of Hosts," *People's Mass Book*,
> #184.

ACCLAMATION AT CONSECRATION:
> (*spoken*) Choice of celebrant from *The English-Latin
> Sacramentary*.

THE SERVICE OF COMMUNION

THE "OUR FATHER"

RITE OF PEACE

FRACTION RITE:
> Litany of the "Lamb of God"

SONG:
> "Whatsoever You Do," *People's Mass Book*, #208.

PERIOD OF REFLECTION:
Intermission

THE DISMISSAL RITE

PRAYER OF BENEDICTION:
Eucharistic Liturgies, p. 21.

BLESSING AND DISMISSAL

ANNOUNCEMENTS

RECESSIONAL:
Same as Processional.

FIRST SUNDAY OF LENT I

Theme: A Time for Suffering

THE ENTRANCE RITE

PROCESSIONAL:
"We Gather Together," *People's Mass Book,* #53.

GREETING:
Eucharistic Liturgies, p. 23.

PENITENTIAL RITE:
(*Response:* Lord, have mercy.)
In sorrow for the times when we have chosen the comfort
of silence rather than the cross of decision, let us pray
to the Lord:
In sorrow for the times when we have resisted Christ's
efforts through the Church to raise us up to new life—a life
of concern and involvement, let us pray to the Lord:
In sorrow for the times when ambition and greed have
caused us to obscure truth by seeking others' approval
through greed and dishonesty at the cost of another person's
dignity, let us pray to the Lord:
In sorrow for intolerance, for having bred suspicion and
casting doubt about another's sincerity, let us pray to the
Lord:

PRAYER OF INVOCATION:
Eucharistic Liturgies, p. 23.

THE SERVICE OF THE WORD

FIRST READING:
Genesis 6:5–7; 8:21a–22. These two passages are linked by
this summary: "And with this begins the story of Noah,
whereby Yahweh promised to rid the earth of evil by the
waters of the flood. At the end of the deluge, Yahweh spoke:
'Never again will I curse. . . .'"

50

RESPONSE:

> Down we sit, marked with dust—the dust of the earth, never
> again to be delicate and tender; now resistant and
> toughened by sinfulness, hardly to be recognized as the
> image and likeness of God.
> Our Redeemer, "the Lord" is his name, says: "Sit in silence
> and creep into shadows. I was angry with my people,
> I had profaned my heritage; I had surrendered it into
> your hands."
> The waters of the flood have touched us in baptism; we
> seek to share in the justification of Noah's family.
> Having come to life in your Son, through the flood of baptism,
> help us now through your Word to walk in his paths
> forever.
> *(All but the last two sentences are taken or adapted from
> Isaiah 47:1–6.)*

SECOND READING:

> 2 Corinthians 6:1–10.

RESPONSE:

> Louis Evely in *Listen to Love*, p. 80.

THE GOSPEL:

> Luke 9:23–26.

GOSPEL ACCLAMATION:

> John 12:23–24, starting, "Now the hour has come. . . ."

HOMILY

GENERAL INTENTIONS:

> (*Response:* Lord, hear our prayer.)
> Selection of intentions from *Your Word Is Near*, pp. 141–142.

PERIOD OF REFLECTION:

> Intermission

PROCESSIONAL:

> "Praise the Lord, O Heavens," *People's Mass Book*, #181.

PRAYER OF BLESSING OVER GIFTS:
Eucharistic Liturgies, p. 24.

THE TABLE PRAYER

PREFACE:
It is right and just for us to give thanks to you, Holy Father, through your Son Jesus Christ, especially during these forty days of renewal and penance.

For we who have so often chosen a way of death and darkness now seek to renew our purpose and our faith.

It is with hope that we have listened to your Word, and now look into ourselves in order to set aside once and for all those thoughts and deeds which have held us back and dimmed our anticipation of your kingdom.

Seeking life without end, a life of peace and joy, we look forward to the day of resurrection.

Joining with all the saints and angels, we sing a hymn to your glory:

HYMN OF PRAISE:
"Praise to the Lord," *People's Mass Book,* #175.

ACCLAMATION AT CONSECRATION:
"Keep in Mind," *People's Mass Book,* #145.

THE SERVICE OF COMMUNION

THE "OUR FATHER"

RITE OF PEACE

FRACTION RITE:
Litany of the "Lamb of God"

SONG:
"Yes, I Shall Arise," *People's Mass Book,* #174.

PERIOD OF REFLECTION:
Intermission

THE DISMISSAL RITE

PRAYER OF BENEDICTION:
Eucharistic Liturgies, p. 24.

BLESSING AND DISMISSAL

ANNOUNCEMENTS

RECESSIONAL:
"All Glory, Praise, and Honor," *People's Mass Book,* #29.

SECOND SUNDAY OF LENT I

Theme: A Season for Every Purpose Under Heaven

THE ENTRANCE RITE

INVITATION TO WORSHIP AND PROCESSIONAL:
All read together lyrics from "Turn, Turn, Turn" by Pete Seeger.

GREETING:
Eucharistic Liturgies, p. 25.

PENITENTIAL RITE:
(*Response:* Lord, have mercy.)
In sorrow for being complacent, we pray to the Lord:
In sorrow for passing judgments about others' intentions and efforts, we pray to the Lord:
In sorrow for waste and the disregard we sometimes have for the earth and all creation, we pray to the Lord:
In sorrow for the times when we have disregarded another's feelings in order to preserve our own comfort and gain, we pray to the Lord:

PRAYER OF INVOCATION:
Eucharistic Liturgies, p. 25.

THE SERVICE OF THE WORD

FIRST READING:
Genesis 12:1–7a.

RESPONSE:
Micah 7:18–20.

SECOND READING:
2 Timothy 1:8–10a.

GOSPEL ACCLAMATION:
"Grant to Us" (Jer. 31:31–34), *Biblical Hymns and Psalms,*
p. 40.

THE GOSPEL:
Mark 9:2–8.

HOMILY

GENERAL INTENTIONS:
Selection from pp. 64–65, *Your Word Is Near,* after which
the celebrant prays, "God, you did not display yourself,"
p. 66 of the same source.

PERIOD OF REFLECTION:
Intermission

PROCESSIONAL:
"Praise the Lord, O Heavens," second verse, *People's Mass
Book,* #181.

PRAYER OF BLESSING OVER GIFTS:
Eucharistic Liturgies, p. 26. May be abbreviated by omitting
first and third sentences.

THE TABLE PRAYER

PREFACE:
Preface for Lent in *The English-Latin Sacramentary.*

HYMN OF PRAISE:
"Praise God, From Whom All Blessings Flow," *People's Mass
Book,* #45.

ACCLAMATION AT CONSECRATION:
"Keep in Mind," *People's Mass Book,* #145.

THE SERVICE OF COMMUNION

THE "OUR FATHER"

RITE OF PEACE

FRACTION RITE:
Litany of the "Lamb of God"

SONG:
"At the Lamb's High Feast We Sing," *Our Parish Prays and Sings,* #2.

PERIOD OF REFLECTION:
Intermission

THE DISMISSAL RITE

PRAYER OF BENEDICTION:
Eucharistic Liturgies, p. 26. First and second sentences may be combined and shortened.

BLESSING AND DISMISSAL

ANNOUNCEMENTS

RECESSIONAL:
"Behold Among Men," *Biblical Hymns and Psalms,* p. 36.

THIRD SUNDAY OF LENT I

Theme: A Celebration of Diversity and Unity in Man

THE ENTRANCE RITE

PROCESSIONAL:
"Hear, O Lord," *Hymnal for Young Christians*, Complete edition, p. 78.

GREETING:
All of "The Preparation" in "The Eucharistic Liturgy," *The Experimental Liturgy Book*, p. 175.

PENITENTIAL RITE:
The proof of God's amazing love is this: it was while we were sinners that Christ died for us. It is in the same Jesus, because we have faith in him, that we dare to approach God with confidence. Let us admit our guilt before our Father.
(*Response:* Lord, have mercy.)
For the times when preoccupation with our own ideas has closed us to the thoughts of others, we pray to the Lord:
For the times we have spoken when it would have been better to remain silent, we pray to the Lord:
For the times we were silent when it would have been well to speak, we pray to the Lord:
For the times we have stifled diversity by our ridicule, our non-attentiveness, our uncharitable criticism, we pray to the Lord:
For the times we have failed to use opportunities to discover and to understand what others believe and why they believe, we pray to the Lord:

PRAYER OF INVOCATION:
"Prayer of St. Francis," *Discovery in Prayer*, p. 99.

THE SERVICE OF THE WORD

FIRST READING:
Dietrich Bonhoeffer in *Listen to Love*, p. 53.

RESPONSE:
Woodrow Wilson in *Listen to Love*, p. 212.

SECOND READING:
Romans 8:18–23, 31a, 35a, 38–39.

RESPONSE:
"Grant to Us" (Jer. 31:31–34), *Biblical Hymns and Psalms*, p. 40.

THE GOSPEL:
Luke 11:14–23; 27–28.

HOMILY

GENERAL INTENTIONS:
   (*Response:* Lord, hear our prayer.)
   That we who dare to call God our Father would also understand that we must accept each man as our brother, we pray to the Lord:
   That we who offer our gifts at this altar would first be reconciled in our hearts and later, in practice, with our brother, we pray to the Lord:
   That we who seek the peace of Christ and the life of the Father would extend our peace and share our life with all our brothers, we pray to the Lord:
   That we who eat bread together in this sacred meal of the Eucharist would share all that we are with one another in patience, in understanding, in forgiveness, we pray to the Lord:

PERIOD OF REFLECTION:
Intermission

PROCESSIONAL:
"They'll Know We Are Christians," *Hymnal for Young Christians*, p. 132.

PRAYER OF BLESSING OVER GIFTS:
> Father, we offer you these many pieces of bread on the one
> plate, and these many drops of wine in one cup as a
> sign of our unity even though we are many and diverse
> people.
> May this symbol of unity become a reality in our lives
> by the sharing of this one bread of Jesus, your Son, who
> with you and the Holy Spirit lives as God, forever and
> ever.

THE TABLE PRAYER

PREFACE:
> We thank you, Almighty God, Father of all men, for sharing
> with us the love that makes you one with your Son and
> with the Holy Spirit.
> We ask that we, your people, who come from so many homes
> and varied occupations; we who differ in thought, in
> education, in race and cultural background; we who share
> in different ages and various experiences of life—we ask
> that we who are so different may yet be as one in mind
> and heart with your Son, Jesus.
> Let our voices cry out to you as one as we sing in praise
> of your holy name:
> (First sentence from "Eucharistic Prayer of Human Unity,"
> *The Experimental Liturgy Book*, p. 100.

HYMN OF PRAISE:
> "Holy, Holy, Holy! Lord God Almighty," *People's Mass
> Book*, #184.

ACCLAMATION AT CONSECRATION:
> "Keep in Mind," *People's Mass Book*, #145.

THE SERVICE OF COMMUNION

THE "OUR FATHER"

RITE OF PEACE

FRACTION RITE:
   Litany of the "Lamb of God"

SONG:
   "Behold Among Men," *Biblical Hymns and Psalms,* p. 36.

PERIOD OF REFLECTION:
   Intermission

THE DISMISSAL RITE

PRAYER OF BENEDICTION:
   "God, we break bread for one another," *Your Word Is Near,*
   p. 121. In first line change "break" to "have broken."

BLESSING AND DISMISSAL

ANNOUNCEMENTS

RECESSIONAL:
   "All Glory, Praise, and Honor," *People's Mass Book,* #29.

FOURTH SUNDAY OF LENT I

Theme: "His Mercy Endures Forever"

THE ENTRANCE RITE

PROCESSIONAL:
> "Praise the Lord, O Heavens," second verse, *People's Mass Book*, #181.

GREETING:
> May our Lord Jesus Christ who has brought us peace and reconciled us to one another be with us all as a sign of the Father's faithfulness.

PENITENTIAL RITE:
> Aware of our need for forgiveness and mercy, let us pause to remember our sins:
> (*Response:* Lord, have mercy.)
> For our tendency to judge one another with superficial values, let us pray to the Lord:
> Because of our inability to admit mistakes in the face of truth, let us pray to the Lord:
> Because of times when we harbor resentment and refuse to forget as well as forgive, let us pray to the Lord:
> For occasions when we have despaired of God's mercy and not sought the forgiveness which he offers us through his Son's living members, let us pray to the Lord:

PRAYER OF INVOCATION:
> "Lord God, we must forgive," *Your Word Is Near*, p. 134.

THE SERVICE OF THE WORD

FIRST READING:
> Hosea 14:2–3; 5–9. Introduction: The first reading today is taken from the concluding chapter of the book of Hosea. This book narrates the story of Hosea and his wife, Gomer. The

61

prophet Hosea has taken the harlot, Gomer, for his wife; but she is repeatedly unfaithful to him. However by God's grace, Hosea accepts her back every time she seeks his forgiveness. Through the prophecy, we learn that Hosea is a figure of God, and his wife is a figure of God's people, who are repeatedly sinful and unfaithful. The mercy that Hosea shows to his wife is an example of the mercy that God has for the people he has chosen for his own.

RESPONSE:
Hosea 14:10.

SECOND READING:
Isaiah 43:1a–3a; 44:3–4.

RESPONSE:
Isaiah 44:23. Adapt last sentence thus: "For God, our Father, has redeemed us and shown his glory among us."

GOSPEL ACCLAMATION:
"Grant to Us" (Jer. 31:31–34), *Biblical Hymns and Psalms*, p. 40.

THE GOSPEL:
Luke 8:1–11.

HOMILY

GENERAL INTENTIONS:
(*Response:* Merciful Father, hear our prayer.)
Selection from pp. 125–127, *Your Word Is Near*. Use first two sentences of "Let us thank the Lord," p. 127 of the same source, for concluding prayer.

PERIOD OF REFLECTION:
Intermission

PROCESSIONAL:
"Behold Among Men," *Biblical Hymns and Psalms*, p. 36.

PRAYER OF BLESSING OVER GIFTS:
"We ask you for bread and for peace," *Your Word Is Near,*
p. 139.

THE TABLE PRAYER

PREFACE:
It is right and just for us to give you thanks, Almighty God,
for you have shown us your mercy and fidelity in the person
of your Son Jesus Christ.
It is especially good for us to give you thanks during this
season of renewal as we seek to know ourselves in the light
of your Gospel and the image of your Son.
Grateful for what you have accomplished in us and for what
you make possible for us to accomplish united with one
another in your Son, we join with all creation as we sing a
hymn to your glory:

HYMN OF PRAISE:
"Holy, Holy, Holy," *People's Mass Book,* #106.

ACCLAMATION AT CONSECRATION:
"Keep in Mind," *People's Mass Book,* #145.

THE SERVICE OF COMMUNION

THE "OUR FATHER"

RITE OF PEACE

FRACTION RITE:
Litany of the "Lamb of God"

SONG:
"Yes, I Shall Arise," *People's Mass Book,* #174.

PERIOD OF REFLECTION:
Intermission

THE DISMISSAL RITE

PRAYER OF BENEDICTION:
> Father of mercy, you have fed us with the bread of heaven,
> and we have accepted this gift of your Son.
> May we never fail to call upon you for mercy.
> Do not let us project our unfaithfulness upon you.
> Help us to remember that when we fail to forgive, you do
> not fail.
> Let us be a sign to those who have despaired and lost
> confidence in your forgiveness that they may find in our
> gentleness and patience, a sign of your mercy and an
> invitation to life in your Son.
> We ask this in his name, who lives with the Spirit forever
> and ever.

BLESSING AND DISMISSAL

ANNOUNCEMENTS

RECESSIONAL:
> "A Mighty Fortress Is Our God," *People's Mass Book,* #187.

FIFTH SUNDAY OF LENT I

Theme: "With the Lord Is Fullness of Redemption"

THE ENTRANCE RITE

PROCESSIONAL:
"Yes, I Shall Arise," *People's Mass Book*, #174.

GREETING:
Eucharistic Liturgies, p. 31.

PENITENTIAL RITE:
Recalling that the Christ who suffered and died for us suffers still in our midst, let us pause to remember our sins:
Reader: Lord, we have sinned against you.
People: Lord, have mercy.
Reader: Lord, show us your mercy and love.
People: Grant us your salvation.

PRAYER OF INVOCATION:
Eucharistic Liturgies, p. 31.

THE SERVICE OF THE WORD

FIRST READING:
Ezekiel 37:12–14.

RESPONSE:
Psalm 130:1–2, 3–4, 5–6, 7–8 (by reader). "With the Lord there is mercy and fullness of redemption" (*by people— alternated with verses from Ps. 130, above*).

SECOND READING:
Romans 8:8–11.

GOSPEL ACCLAMATION:
"Grant to Us" (Jer. 31:31–34), *Biblical Hymns and Psalms*, p. 40.

THE GOSPEL:
John 11:1–44.

HOMILY

GENERAL INTENTIONS:
(*Response:* Lord, hear our prayer.)
Selection from *Your Word Is Near,* pp. 98–99, followed by
"You are the voice of the living God," p. 97 of the same
source.

PERIOD OF REFLECTION:
Intermission

PROCESSIONAL:
"Hear, O Lord," *Hymnal for Young Christians,* p. 78.

PRAYER OF BLESSING OVER GIFTS:
Eucharistic Liturgies, p. 32.

THE TABLE PRAYER

PREFACE:
Preface for the Passion and the Holy Cross from *The
English-Latin Sacramentary.*

HYMN OF PRAISE:
"Praise to the Lord," *People's Mass Book,* #175.

ACCLAMATION AT CONSECRATION:
"Keep in Mind," *People's Mass Book,* #145.

THE SERVICE OF COMMUNION

THE "OUR FATHER"

RITE OF PEACE

FRACTION RITE:
Litany of the "Lamb of God"

SONG:
"God Is Love," *Hymnal for Young Christians,* p. 95.

PERIOD OF REFLECTION:
Intermission

THE DISMISSAL RITE

PRAYER OF BENEDICTION:
Eucharistic Liturgies, p. 32.

BLESSING AND DISMISSAL

ANNOUNCEMENTS

RECESSIONAL:
"O Sacred Head Surrounded," *People's Mass Book,* #27.

———

An alternate to the Service of the Word in the foregoing liturgy
is the Stations of the Cross, consisting of Scripture readings and
prayers composed by families of children in the Sunday school
program of the parish or by any other group of families that would
be attending the same Sunday liturgy. The Scripture readings
originally used are given below. Note that after the naming of
each station some background should be given by the minister
leading the service, as the Scripture passage selected (sometimes
a paraphrase or a reflection) is not always a narrative of the
event represented by a particular station. The people's response
to each prayer is "Help me to know what you meant here." The
song "Whatsoever You Do," *People's Mass Book,* #208, is sung
after every other station (excluding the fourteenth) and after
the concluding prayer. The liturgy then continues with the
General Intentions and Procession of Gifts.

1. Jesus Is Condemned
   Scripture: John 10:17–18. (At each station the "Scripture
   reading" is followed by the prayer and the people's response.)

2. Jesus Takes Up His Cross
   Scripture: Matthew 25:42–43.
3. Jesus Falls the First Time
   "Scripture": How human in his weakness is the Son of Man.
   My Father willed it thus. I could not be your model
   otherwise. If you would be my other self, you also must accept
   without complaint your human frailties.
4. Jesus Meets His Mother
   Scripture: Luke 2:33–35.
5. Simon Helps Jesus
   Scripture: Matthew 25:45.
6. Veronica Helps Jesus
   "Scripture": Where is my face, you ask? At home whenever
   eyes fill up with tears, at work when tensions rise, on
   playgrounds, in the slums, the courts, the hospitals, the jails
   —wherever suffering exists—my face is there. And there I look
   for you to wipe away my blood and tears.
7. Jesus Falls Again
   Scripture: Matthew 5:11–12.
8. Jesus Consoles the Women
   "Scripture": How often had I longed to take the children of
   Jerusalem and gather them to me. But they refused. But now
   these women weep for me and my heart mourns for them—
   mourns for their sorrows that will come.
9. The Third Fall
   Scripture: Romans 5:12.
10. Jesus Is Stripped
    Scripture: Ephesians 4:23–25.
11. Jesus Is Crucified
    Scripture: John 3:16.
12. Jesus Dies
    Scripture: Romans 6:2a–5.
13. Jesus Is Taken Down from the Cross
    "Scripture": The sacrifice is done. Yes, my Mass is complete;
    but not my mother's and not yours, my other self. My mother
    still must cradle in her arms the lifeless body of the Son she
    bore. You, too, must part from those you love, and grief
    will come to you.

14. **Jesus Is Buried**
    Scripture: John 12:26.
15. **Resurrection**
    Scripture: John 14:18–19, followed by this injunction: "Go now! Take up your cross and with your life, complete your way."

PALM SUNDAY

Theme: Jesus Christ, Sovereign King and Man of Sorrows

THE ENTRANCE RITE

PROCESSIONAL:
"To Jesus Christ Our Sovereign King," *People's Mass Book*, #48.

GREETING AND PENITENTIAL RITE:
Eucharistic Liturgies, pp. 33–34; people join in prayer, "Father, so often we are foolish. . . ."

PRAYER OF INVOCATION:
"Lord God, you sent your Son into this world," *Your Word Is Near*, p. 59.

THE SERVICE OF THE WORD

FIRST READING:
Isaiah 49:1–3, 5a–7, 13–16a.

RESPONSE:
"For Baby" by John Denver. *(May be recited by reader or sung by cantor.)*

EXIT PROCESSIONAL:
"He Was Led Like A Sheep" or other appropriate number is sung by choir as congregation moves to the site selected for Blessing of Palms.

ANTIPHON:
"Hosanna to the Son of David!" The priest prays this line; the people respond with the entirety of the antiphon as found in *The English-Latin Sacramentary*, Palm Sunday.

BLESSING OF PALMS:
Follows the above in *The English-Latin Sacramentary*.

THE GOSPEL:
Matthew 21:1–9.

RESPONSE:
(read while palms are distributed)
Ps. 24:1–2, 7, 8, 10 *(by reader)*.
"The Hebrew people, bearing olive branches, went to meet
the Lord, crying aloud, and saying, 'Hosanna!'" *(by people
—alternated with verses of Ps. 24, above)*.

PROCESSIONAL:
*(Sung during Procession of Palms, which brings congregation
back into the church for remainder of liturgy; as many of
the following as needed may be used.)*
"All Glory, Praise, and Honor," *People's Mass Book*, #29.
"Battle Hymn of the Republic," *People's Mass Book*, #234.
"Sion, Sing," *People's Mass Book*, #165.

THE READING OF THE PASSION:
Mark 14:32–72; 15:1–46.

HOMILY:
(if time allows)

PERIOD OF REFLECTION:
Intermission

PROCESSIONAL:
"Yes, I Shall Arise," *People's Mass Book*, #174.

PRAYER OF BLESSING OVER GIFTS:
Eucharistic Liturgies, p. 34. Omit first two sentences.

THE TABLE PRAYER

PREFACE:
Preface for the Passion and the Holy Cross in *The
English-Latin Sacramentary*.

HYMN OF PRAISE:

"Holy, Holy, Holy! Lord God Almighty," second verse,
People's Mass Book, #184.

THE SERVICE OF COMMUNION

THE "OUR FATHER"

RITE OF PEACE

FRACTION RITE:
Litany of the "Lamb of God"

SONG:
"Priestly People," *People's Mass Book,* #146.

PERIOD OF REFLECTION:
Intermission

THE DISMISSAL RITE

PRAYER OF BENEDICTION:
Eucharistic Liturgies, p. 35. Omit second and third sentences.

BLESSING AND DISMISSAL

ANNOUNCEMENTS

RECESSIONAL:
"All Glory, Praise, and Honor," *People's Mass Book,* #29.

HOLY THURSDAY I

Theme: Celebration of the Lord's Supper

THE ENTRANCE RITE

PROCESSIONAL:
"The King of Glory," *Hymnal for Young Christians*, p. 60.

GREETING AND PRAYER OF INVOCATION:
Eucharistic Liturgies, p. 36.

THE SERVICE OF THE WORD

FIRST READING:
"What Are We Fed," *St. Andrew's Bible Missal*, p. 422.

RESPONSE:
"Let It Be," first verse, by John Lennon and Paul McCartney.

SECOND READING:
1 Corinthians 11:17–34.

RESPONSE:
"Let It Be," second verse (*continuation of first response*).

THE GOSPEL:
John 13:1–17.

HOMILY

WASHING OF THE FEET:
Introduction by reader:
This evening for the washing of the feet various representative
members of the parish family have been selected to participate
in the ceremony. As the priest washes the feet of these people,
he is reminded of the service he is to render to all the members
of the parish. At the same time, all of us are given an example
as to how we are to render service to one another and to all
men.

73

SONG:
   "Whatsoever You Do," *People's Mass Book,* #208.

RITE OF RECONCILIATION:
   (During Preparation of Gifts) *Eucharistic Liturgies,* p. 37.

PRAYER OF BLESSING OVER GIFTS:
   Eucharistic Liturgies, p. 37.

THE TABLE PRAYER

THE SERVICE OF COMMUNION

THE "OUR FATHER"

RITE OF PEACE

FRACTION RITE:
   Litany of the "Lamb of God." During this rite today the prayer
   "We break bread together," *Eucharistic Liturgies,* p. 41, is
   said by the celebrant.

SONG:
   "They'll Know We Are Christians," *Hymnal for Young
   Christians,* p. 132.

PERIOD OF REFLECTION:
   Intermission
   Reading for Meditation: John 6:53–58.

THE DISMISSAL RITE

PRAYER OF BENEDICTION:
   Eucharistic Liturgies, p. 42. Omit first sentence; begin second
   with address, "Father."

BLESSING AND DISMISSAL:
   Blessing in *Eucharistic Liturgies,* p. 42.

ANNOUNCEMENTS

RECESSIONAL:
    "Whatsoever You Do," *People's Mass Book,* #208.

GOOD FRIDAY

Theme: "It Is Finished"

All of this liturgy is taken from *Eucharistic Liturgies,* pp. 43–55.

Music: In response to "Behold the wood of the Cross . . ." the people sing, "Come, let us adore." Immediately afterward— and before veneration of the Cross by the congregation— "Bridge Over Troubled Waters" by Simon and Garfunkel is sung. The celebrant introduces the song with an explanation of its significance in relation to the Cross.

"O Sacred Head Surrounded," *People's Mass Book,* #27, is sung while the celebrant goes to the altar of repose for the consecrated bread and wine. "My Shepherd Is the Lord" (Ps. 22, Antiphon I), *Twenty-Four Psalms and a Canticle,* p. 10, is sung during Communion.

A significant reading to print on the program for meditation is from Pierre Babin, *Listen to Love,* p. 83.

EASTER VIGIL I

Theme: "Let Every Heart Be Glad and Rejoice"

THE SERVICE OF THE WORD

PROCESSIONAL:
  "Yes, I Shall Arise," *People's Mass Book*, #174.

GREETING:
  Blessings and peace to you from our Lord, Jesus Christ,
    who through his death has brought us to life.

FIRST READING:
  Genesis 1:1 to 2:3 (division of reading between reader and
  celebrant as in *Eucharistic Liturgies*, pp. 58–60).

RESPONSE:
  "O God, Our Help in Ages Past," *People's Mass Book*, #185.

SECOND READING:
  Exodus 14:19–25, 27–29.

LIGHTING OF PASCHAL CANDLE:
  Eucharistic Liturgies, p. 61.

RESPONSE:
  "To Jesus Christ, Our Sovereign King," *People's Mass Book*,
  #48.

THE GOSPEL:
  John 4:7–15a.

Blessing of Water, Renewal of Baptismal Vows, Administering
of Baptism: New Baptismal Rite, Chapter Two, *Manual of
Celebration*, pp. 13–23.

  (After the anointing before baptism, the people welcome

77

*those to be baptized by reading the following prayer and
Gospel passage.)*
The faith we wish to share with you is not a hidden, secret
faith of a buried Christ, but faith in a living Christ—risen
from the dead. Therefore, we break from this place, as
Christ broke from the tomb, and lead you to new life in
the Spirit. The risen Christ, after his resurrection, was always
recognized by his believers in the breaking of bread; so
now we lead you to him as we share his Body and Blood.
Gospel passage is from Matthew 28:1–7a.
*(If the service began in the basement of the church or in
an adjoining building, the congregation, led by the
minister and those to be baptized, now move to the
church. The ministers and those to be baptized go to the
front; the others gather around or face the font from their
pews. The Baptismal Rite continues.)*

PERIOD OF REFLECTION:
   Intermission

PROCESSIONAL:
   "Jesus Christ Is Risen Today," *People's Mass Book,* #30.

PRAYER OF BLESSING OVER GIFTS:
   Eucharistic Liturgies, p. 63.

THE TABLE PRAYER

PREFACE:
   Preface for Easter, *The English-Latin Sacramentary.*

HYMN OF PRAISE:
   "Holy, Holy, Holy! Lord God of Hosts," *People's Mass Book,*
   #184.

ACCLAMATION AT CONSECRATION:
   "Keep in Mind," *People's Mass Book,* #145.

THE SERVICE OF COMMUNION

THE "OUR FATHER"

RITE OF PEACE

FRACTION RITE:
Litany of the "Lamb of God"

SONG:
"Priestly People," *People's Mass Book*, #146.

PERIOD OF REFLECTION:
Intermission

THE DISMISSAL RITE

PRAYER OF BENEDICTION:
Eucharistic Liturgies, p. 65.

THE EXSULTET:
As in *The English-Latin Sacramentary*.

BLESSING AND DISMISSAL:
Blessing as in *Eucharistic Liturgies*, p. 65.

ANNOUNCEMENTS

RECESSIONAL:
"Rejoice, The Lord Is King," *Hymnal for Young Christians*,
p. 115.

EASTER SUNDAY I

Theme: "He Is Risen"

THE ENTRANCE RITE

PROCESSIONAL:
"Jesus Christ Is Risen Today," *People's Mass Book*, #30.

GREETING:
Eucharistic Liturgies, p. 66.

PRAYER OF INVOCATION:
Eucharistic Liturgies, p. 66.

THE SERVICE OF THE WORD

FIRST READING:
Revelation 21:1–4.

RESPONSE:
"Behold Among Men," *Biblical Hymns and Psalms*, p. 36.

SECOND READING:
Acts 10:34, 37–43.

RESPONSE:
Ps. 118:1–2, 22–23 (*by reader*).
Ps. 118:24 (*by people—alternated with verses given above*).

THE GOSPEL:
John 20:1–9.

GOSPEL ACCLAMATION:
(*Spoken*) Alleluia, Christ has become our Paschal sacrifice:
let us feast with joy in the Lord, Alleluia!

HOMILY

GENERAL INTENTIONS:
  Selection from pp. 85–87, *Your Word Is Near.*

PERIOD OF REFLECTION:
  Intermission

PROCESSIONAL:
  "At the Lamb's High Feast," *Our Parish Prays and Sings,* #2.

PRAYER OF BLESSING OVER GIFTS:
  Eucharistic Liturgies, p. 67.

THE TABLE PRAYER

PREFACE:
  Preface for Easter, *The English-Latin Sacramentary.*

HYMN OF PRAISE:
  "Praise God, From Whom All Blessings Flow," *People's Mass Book,* #45.

ACCLAMATION AT CONSECRATION:
  "Keep in Mind," *People's Mass Book,* #145.

THE SERVICE OF COMMUNION

THE "OUR FATHER"

RITE OF PEACE

FRACTION RITE:
  Litany of the "Lamb of God"

SONG:
  "O Sons and Daughters of the Lord," *People's Mass Book,* #32.

PERIOD OF REFLECTION:
  Intermission

THE DISMISSAL RITE

PRAYER OF BENEDICTION:
   Eucharistic Liturgies, p. 67.

BLESSING AND DISMISSAL

ANNOUNCEMENTS

RECESSIONAL:
   "Christ the Lord Is Risen Today," *People's Mass Book,* #31.

SECOND SUNDAY OF EASTER I

Theme: A Celebration of Ministry

THE ENTRANCE RITE

PROCESSIONAL:
"We Gather Together," *People's Mass Book,* #53.

GREETING:
Blessings and Peace to you from our Lord Jesus Christ who
has risen from the dead and who dies now no more.

PRAYER OF INVOCATION:
Father, your Son and faithful servant brought healing to those
who were sick, words of comfort to those who were in need.
And they killed him, hanging him on a tree.
We now seek to walk the path he walked before us.
We must speak peace when men cry in pain, bring healing
to the wounds that scar our world.
And we too must die with him.
But you raised him up to life, and so promise to raise us with
him.
This is the message we have heard; this is the message we
preach.
May our hope in you never grow dim.
All glory be to you Father, now and forever.
(Adapted from *Eucharistic Liturgies,* p. 68.)

THE SERVICE OF THE WORD

FIRST READING:
Isaiah 6:1–7.

RESPONSE:
"Alleluia, Alleluia, Alleluia" from "O Sons and Daughters,"
People's Mass Book, #32.

SECOND READING:
Acts 6:1–6.

GOSPEL ACCLAMATION:
"Alleluia, Alleluia, Alleluia," cited above.

THE GOSPEL:
John 13:2–5, 12–15, 17–20.

GOSPEL ACCLAMATION:
(*Spoken*) Alleluia, whoever welcomes the one I send welcomes me, and whoever welcomes me welcomes the one who sent me. Alleluia.

HOMILY

PERIOD OF REFLECTION:
Intermission

PROCESSIONAL:
"Christ the Lord Is Risen Today," *People's Mass Book*, #31.

PRAYER OF BLESSING OVER GIFTS:
Accept the gifts of your joyous Church, O Lord; you have given her cause for such joy; grant that we may always maintain this happiness and joy as a sign to others that you are risen and living among us.
We ask this through your Son, Jesus, who lives together with the Holy Spirit, forever and ever.

THE TABLE PRAYER

PREFACE:
Preface for Easter, *The English-Latin Sacramentary*.

HYMN OF PRAISE:
"Holy, Holy, Holy! Lord God Almighty," *People's Mass Book*, #184.

ACCLAMATION AT CONSECRATION:
"Keep in Mind," *People's Mass Book,* #145.

THE SERVICE OF COMMUNION

THE "OUR FATHER"

RITE OF PEACE

FRACTION RITE:
Litany of the "Lamb of God"

SONG:
"Peace, My Friends," *Hymnal for Young Christians,* Vol. II,
p. 34.

PERIOD OF REFLECTION:
Intermission

THE DISMISSAL RITE

PRAYER OF BENEDICTION:
Eucharistic Liturgies, p. 69.

BLESSING AND DISMISSAL

ANNOUNCEMENTS

RECESSIONAL:
"A Mighty Fortress," *People's Mass Book,* #187.

THIRD SUNDAY OF EASTER I

Theme: A Pilgrim People

THE ENTRANCE RITE

INVITATION TO WORSHIP:

We are all seekers, looking for that something or someone
who will conclude our searching for whatever it is we are
looking for. When the bishops of the Second Vatican Council
told us we were "pilgrims," the term was new, but the
experience is as old as man. Call it "pilgrimage"; call it
"search"; call it "questioning or wandering"—we are all on
the way. Today, as Christian people, we gather to reflect on
our own personal pilgrimage, our own seeking for life and
whatever it holds for us. We do this as a people joined
together in the breaking of bread.

PROCESSIONAL:

"Alleluia, Sing to Jesus," *The Hymnal of the Protestant
Episcopal Church in the United States of America,* #347.

GREETING:

May God our Father who has called us to himself through
his Son, Jesus, be with us all, and by their Holy Spirit
may we have the courage to continue our journey in life.

PRAYER OF INVOCATION:

Our Father in heaven, believing in your goodness, we dare
to hope for an ever greater fulfillment in life.
But sometimes, Father, our looking and searching is obscured;
our own desires and ideas of life become so strong that we
tend to forget the kind of life your Son promised us.
Father, by the strength of your Spirit and the word of your
Son, may we once again focus our eyes on the life you
have promised us both now and in time to come.
We ask all this in your Son's name, who with you and the
Spirit lives as God, forever and ever.

86

THE SERVICE OF THE WORD

FIRST READING:
Acts 2:14a, 22–28.

RESPONSE:
Ps. 16:1, 5, 7–8, 9–10, 11 (*by reader*). "Lord, you will show us the path of life" (*Ps. 16:1, adapted; read by people alternately with verses given above*).

SECOND READING:
1 Peter 1:17–21.

GOSPEL ACCLAMATION:
"Alleluia! The Strife Is O'er," first verse, *People's Mass Book,* #34.

THE GOSPEL:
Luke 24:13–25.

GOSPEL ACCLAMATION:
"Alleluia! The Strife Is O'er," cited above, third verse.

HOMILY

GENERAL INTENTIONS:
(*Response:* Risen Savior, hear our prayer).
(*First two petitions should ask blessing relative to some current national, state, or local event or problem.*)
For the poor that they may not despair; for the downtrodden that they may react creatively; for those who hold differing opinions that they may learn to listen and to have mutual respect, we pray to the Lord:
For ourselves, that by our hearing God's Word and reflecting upon it and by the support we receive in coming together here to break bread, we may find the strength to welcome all that life brings to us and respond to it in a hopeful manner, we pray to the Lord:

PERIOD OF REFLECTION:
   Intermission

PROCESSIONAL:
   "Ye Watchers and Ye Holy Ones," *The Hymnal of the
   Protestant Episcopal Church in the United States of
   America*, #599.

PRAYER OF BLESSING OVER GIFTS:
   Eucharistic Liturgies, p. 73. Omit fifth sentence.

THE TABLE PRAYER

PREFACE:
   Preface for Easter, *The English-Latin Sacramentary.*

HYMN OF PRAISE:
   "Sing Praise to Our Creator," *People's Mass Book*, #43.

ACCLAMATION AT CONSECRATION:
   (*Spoken*) "Lord, by your cross and resurrection . . ." from
   The English-Latin Sacramentary.

THE SERVICE OF COMMUNION

THE "OUR FATHER"

RITE OF PEACE

FRACTION RITE:
   Litany of the "Lamb of God"

SONG:
   "At the Lamb's High Feast," *Our Parish Prays and Sings*, #2.

PERIOD OF REFLECTION:
   Intermission

THE DISMISSAL RITE

PRAYER OF BENEDICTION:
> Blessed are you, Father.
> May we who have shared this meal be stripped of everything
> that is false, of every form of artificiality which hides our
> own true selves.
> Thus may we travel together on our journey toward you in
> openness and honesty, free to be ourselves and free to be
> your sons.
> We ask this in the name of your Son, Jesus Christ, who is
> the Lord in heaven and on earth, now and forever.

BLESSING AND DISMISSAL

ANNOUNCEMENTS

RECESSIONAL:
> "A Mighty Fortress," *People's Mass Book*, #187.

FOURTH SUNDAY OF EASTER I

Theme: "My Shepherd Is the Lord"

THE ENTRANCE RITE

PROCESSIONAL:
"My Shepherd Is the Lord" (Ps. 22, Antiphon I), *Twenty-Four Psalms and a Canticle*, p. 10.

GREETING:
Eucharistic Liturgies, p. 74.

PRAYER OF INVOCATION:
Eucharistic Liturgies, p. 74. Omit third and fourth sentences.

THE SERVICE OF THE WORD

FIRST READING:
1 Peter 2:20b–25.

RESPONSE:
Ps. 118:1, 8–9; 21–23; 26, 28b–29 (*by reader*).
"Through his wounds we have been healed; having died with him, we now live forever" (*by people—alternating with verses from Ps. 118 above*).

SECOND READING:
1 John 3:1–2.

GOSPEL ACCLAMATION:
"Alleluia, The Strife Is O'er," first verse, *People's Mass Book*, #34.

THE GOSPEL:
John 10:11–18.

GOSPEL ACCLAMATION:
"Alleluia, The Strife Is O'er," cited above, third verse.

HOMILY

GENERAL INTENTIONS:
   (*Response:* Risen Savior, hear our prayer.)
   Selection from pp. 142–143, Huub Oosterhuis, *Your Word Is Near.*

PERIOD OF REFLECTION:
   Intermission

PROCESSIONAL:
   "At the Lamb's High Feast," *Our Parish Prays and Sings,* #2.

PRAYER OF BLESSING OVER GIFTS:
   Eucharistic Liturgies, p. 71.

THE TABLE PRAYER

PREFACE:
   Preface for Easter in *The English-Latin Sacramentary* up to
   "restored our life." Add the following:
   Therefore we pledge ourselves to die as he died, for one
      another willingly, and to live as he lived, never to be
      overcome by evil we together can destroy.
   For this we are giving thanks and praise, and so sing together
      with one voice:

HYMN OF PRAISE:
   "Sing Praise to Our Creator," *People's Mass Book,* #43.

ACCLAMATION AT CONSECRATION:
   (*Spoken*) "Dying, you destroyed our death . . ." from *The
   English-Latin Sacramentary.*

THE SERVICE OF COMMUNION

THE "OUR FATHER"

RITE OF PEACE

FRACTION RITE:
Litany of the "Lamb of God"

SONG:
"Alleluia! Sing to Jesus," *The Hymnal of the Protestant Episcopal Church in the United States of America*, #347.

PERIOD OF REFLECTION:
Intermission

THE DISMISSAL RITE

PRAYER OF BENEDICTION:
Eucharistic Liturgies, p. 75. Omit second and third sentences.

BLESSING AND DISMISSAL

ANNOUNCEMENTS

RECESSIONAL:
"Ye Watchers and Ye Holy Ones," *The Hymnal of the Protestant Episcopal Church in the United States of America*, #599.

FIFTH SUNDAY OF EASTER I

Theme: A Celebration of Christian Service

THE ENTRANCE RITE

PROCESSIONAL:
"Ye Watchers and Ye Holy Ones," *The Hymnal of the Protestant Episcopal Church in the United States of America,* #599.

GREETING:
Eucharistic Liturgies, p. 76.

PRAYER OF INVOCATION:
"Let us pray and never cease to ask," *Your Word Is Near,* p. 39.

THE SERVICE OF THE WORD

FIRST READING:
Isaiah 1:11–17.

RESPONSE:
"Reflection for Morning, Twelfth Day," *Free to Live, Free to Die,* p. 47.

SECOND READING:
"On Giving" through the line ". . . the search for one who shall receive is joy greater than giving"; *The Prophet,* pp. 20–21.

GOSPEL ACCLAMATION:
"Alleluia, The Strife Is O'er," first verse, *People's Mass Book,* #34.

THE GOSPEL:
Matthew 25:31–46.

GOSPEL ACCLAMATION:
"Alleluia, The Strife Is O'er," cited above, third verse.

HOMILY

GENERAL INTENTIONS:
(*Response:* Lord, let us see you in our brother.)

For ourselves, that we come to understand that our less
  fortunate brothers will be fed and comforted not by our
  prayers but only through our personal caring and sharing
  in their lives, let us pray to the Lord:

For those in government and in welfare services that their
  work and programs might be designed to alleviate poverty
  and other forms of human suffering, and that we cooperate
  with them in removing the causes of these evils in our
  world, let us pray to the Lord:

For those involved with planning and causing the progress of
  our cities, that while they create marvels of concrete, steel
  and glass, they may never forget that the only true growth
  of man is measured by the ever-greater development of the
  individual person in those cities, let us pray to the Lord:

For those who give of themselves so unselfishly and tirelessly
  in their service to others, and for ourselves, that we may
  share their burdens as a sign of who we are, let us pray
  to the Lord:

PERIOD OF REFLECTION:
Intermission

PROCESSIONAL:
"Whatsoever You Do," *People's Mass Book,* #208.

PRAYER OF BLESSING OVER GIFTS:
Eucharistic Liturgies, p. 77.

THE TABLE PRAYER

PREFACE:
First eleven lines of "Canon of Christian Service," *The
Experimental Liturgy Book,* p. 66. Add the following:
Together with all those in your heavenly kingdom, we sing
in praise of your name:

HYMN OF PRAISE:
"Holy, Holy, Holy! Lord God Almighty," *People's Mass Book,* #184.

ACCLAMATION AT CONSECRATION:
(*Spoken*) "Dying you destroyed our death . . ." from *The English-Latin Sacramentary.*

THE SERVICE OF COMMUNION

THE "OUR FATHER"

RITE OF PEACE

FRACTION RITE:
Litany of the "Lamb of God"

SONG:
"Of My Hands," *Hymnal for Young Christians,* p. 79.

PERIOD OF REFLECTION:
Intermission
Reading for Meditation (*printed on program*): 1 John 3: 1a, 16–17.

THE DISMISSAL RITE

PRAYER OF BENEDICTION:
"Lord God, your kingdom is here," *Your Word Is Near,* p. 104.

BLESSING AND DISMISSAL

ANNOUNCEMENTS

RECESSIONAL:
"They'll Know We Are Christians by Our Love," *Hymnal for Young Christians,* p. 132.

SIXTH SUNDAY OF EASTER I

Theme: Men of the Spirit

THE ENTRANCE RITE

PROCESSIONAL:
"At the Lamb's High Feast," *Our Parish Prays and Sings*, #2.

GREETING:
Eucharistic Liturgies, p. 80.

PRAYER OF INVOCATION:
Eucharistic Liturgies, p. 80.

THE SERVICE OF THE WORD

FIRST READING:
Karl Barth in *Listen to Love*, pp. 170–171, beginning with "When we speak of the Holy Spirit, let us look not at all men . . ." and ending with ". . . when he sends us his Holy Spirit."

RESPONSE:
Silent reflection on the following: "The Tree and the Reed," from *The Fables of Aesop*, reprinted in *Coping*, p. 79.

SECOND READING:
Acts 8:5–8.

GOSPEL ACCLAMATION:
"Alleluia, The Strife Is O'er," first verse, *People's Mass Book*, #34.

THE GOSPEL:
John 14:23–29.

GOSPEL ACCLAMATION:
"Alleluia, The Strife Is O'er," cited above, third verse.

HOMILY

GENERAL INTENTIONS:
   (*Response:* Lord, hear our prayer.)
   Selection from pp. 141–142, Huub Oosterhuis, *Your Word Is Near.*

PROFESSION OF FAITH:
   The Nicene Creed. Introduction:
   Father, through your Spirit, you have given us a new heart.
   Let our hearts be filled with the Spirit of love in a new
   Pentecost, that we may be united with you through our Lord,
   Jesus Christ, so that in this bond we may live out openly
   with courage the faith we now profess:

PERIOD OF REFLECTION:
   Intermission

PROCESSIONAL:
   "We Shall Go Up With Joy" (Ps. 121, Antiphon I),
   Twenty-Four Psalms and a Canticle, p. 42.

PRAYER OF BLESSING OVER GIFTS:
   Eucharistic Liturgies, p. 81. Omit third sentence.

THE TABLE PRAYER

PREFACE:
   Preface for Pentecost in *The English-Latin Sacramentary.*

HYMN OF PRAISE:
   "Sing Praise to Our Creator," third verse, *People's Mass Book,*
   #43.

ACCLAMATION AT CONSECRATION:
   "Keep in Mind," *People's Mass Book,* #145.

THE SERVICE OF COMMUNION

THE "OUR FATHER"

RITE OF PEACE

FRACTION RITE:
Litany of the "Lamb of God"

SONG:
"Alleluia! Sing to Jesus," *The Hymnal of the Protestant Episcopal Church in the United States of America,* #347.

PERIOD OF REFLECTION:
Intermission

THE DISMISSAL RITE

PRAYER OF BENEDICTION:
Eucharistic Liturgies, p. 81.

BLESSING AND DISMISSAL

ANNOUNCEMENTS

RECESSIONAL:
"Ye Watchers and Ye Holy Ones," *The Hymnal of the Protestant Episcopal Church in the United States of America,* #599.

FESTIVAL OF THE ASCENSION I

Theme: "Why Do You Stand Looking Upward?"

THE ENTRANCE RITE

PROCESSIONAL:
"We Gather Together," *People's Mass Book,* #53.

GREETING:
Eucharistic Liturgies, p. 78.

PRAYER OF INVOCATION:
Eucharistic Liturgies, p. 78. Omit third sentence.

THE SERVICE OF THE WORD

FIRST READING:
Acts 1:1–11.

RESPONSE:
"All the Earth" (Ps. 100), *People's Mass Book,* #141.

SECOND READING:
Ephesians 1:17–23.

GOSPEL ACCLAMATION:
"Alleluia, The Strife Is O'er," first verse, *People's Mass Book,* #34.

THE GOSPEL:
Luke 24:46–53.

GOSPEL ACCLAMATION:
"Alleluia, The Strife Is O'er," cited above, third verse.

HOMILY

PERIOD OF REFLECTION:
Intermission

PROCESSIONAL:
"At the Lamb's High Feast," *Our Parish Prays and Sings,* #2.

PRAYER OF BLESSING OVER GIFTS:
Eucharistic Liturgies, p. 79.

THE TABLE PRAYER

PREFACE:
Preface for the Ascension in *The English-Latin Sacramentary.*

HYMN OF PRAISE:
"Praise to the Lord," *People's Mass Book,* #175.

ACCLAMATION AT CONSECRATION:
"Keep in Mind," *People's Mass Book,* #145.

THE SERVICE OF COMMUNION

THE "OUR FATHER"

RITE OF PEACE

FRACTION RITE:
Litany of the "Lamb of God"

SONG:
"Alleluia, Sing to Jesus," *The Hymnal of the Protestant Episcopal Church in the United States of America,* #347.

PERIOD OF REFLECTION:
Intermission

THE DISMISSAL RITE

PRAYER OF BENEDICTION:
Eucharistic Liturgies, p. 79. Omit third sentence.

BLESSING AND DISMISSAL

ANNOUNCEMENTS

RECESSIONAL:
"Let the Earth Rejoice and Sing," *People's Mass Book*, #39.

SUNDAY AFTER ASCENSION I

Theme: Mother's Day

THE ENTRANCE RITE

PROCESSIONAL:
"Send Forth Your Spirit" (Ps. 104), *Biblical Hymns and Psalms*, p. 34.

GREETING:
Eucharistic Liturgies, p. 78.

PRAYER OF INVOCATION:
Eucharistic Liturgies, p. 78. Omit third sentence.

THE SERVICE OF THE WORD

FIRST READING:
Proverbs 31:10–31.

RESPONSE:
"Alleluia! Alleluia!," *Biblical Hymns and Psalms*, p. 86.

THE GOSPEL:
Luke 2:41–52.

GOSPEL ACCLAMATION:
"Alleluia! Alleluia!," cited above.

THIRD READING:
"The Reason My Mother Should Win an Oscar," from *Raymond and Me That Summer*, reprinted in *I've Got A Name*, p. 28. Use only if effective readers are available.

HOMILY

GENERAL INTENTIONS:
(*Response:* Lord, hear our prayer and fill us with your Spirit.)

In loving memory of mothers who have died, let us pray
   to the Lord:
With gratitude to those who are still doing the things that
   only a mother can do best, let us pray to the Lord:
For the safe delivery of those with first child, let us pray
   to the Lord:
For those mothers who are hurt, disappointed, and confused,
   let us pray to the Lord:

PERIOD OF REFLECTION:
   Intermission

PROCESSIONAL:
   "At the Lamb's High Feast," *Our Parish Prays and Sings,* #2.

PRAYER OF BLESSING OVER GIFTS:
   Eucharistic Liturgies, p. 79. Substitute the following for the
   first two sentences:
   Father, we come to you now, not escaping our world, but
   realizing that this world and its condition is our
   responsibility.
   We bring here the needs of all men.

THE TABLE PRAYER

PREFACE:
   First eleven lines from "Canon of Christian Service," *The
   Experimental Liturgy Book,* p. 66. Add the following:
   On this day, we especially offer you our thanks as we celebrate
   Mother's Day;
      for it is by the loving service
      and mercy of mothers that we know
      of your own loving kindness for us.
   And so, with those joined already with you,
      we sing in joy:

HYMN OF PRAISE:
   "Praise God, From Whom All Blessings Flow," *People's Mass
   Book,* #45.

ACCLAMATION AT CONSECRATION:
    "Keep in Mind," *People's Mass Book*, #145.

THE SERVICE OF COMMUNION

THE "OUR FATHER"

RITE OF PEACE

FRACTION RITE:
    Litany of the "Lamb of God"

SONG:
    "Alleluia! Sing to Jesus," *The Hymnal of the Protestant Episcopal Church in the United States of America*, #347.

PERIOD OF REFLECTION:
    Intermission

THE DISMISSAL RITE

PRAYER OF BENEDICTION:
    Eucharistic Liturgies, p. 79. Omit third sentence.

BLESSING AND DISMISSAL

ANNOUNCEMENTS

RECESSIONAL:
    "Let the Earth Rejoice and Sing," *People's Mass Book*, #39.

PENTECOST SUNDAY I

Theme: God Breathes on His People

THE ENTRANCE RITE

INVITATION TO WORSHIP:
   Acts 2:1–8, 12.

PROCESSIONAL:
   "Send Forth Your Spirit" (Ps. 104), *Biblical Hymns and Psalms,* p. 34.

GREETING:
   The Spirit of the Lord is upon us; he has anointed us to
      preach good news to the poor and to bring hope to the
      discouraged.
   (Adapted from *Eucharistic Liturgies,* p. 82.)

PRAYER OF INVOCATION:
   Eucharistic Liturgies, p. 82. May be abbreviated by leaving
   out second and third sentences.

THE SERVICE OF THE WORD

FIRST READING:
   A New Catechism, pp. 193–194. Begin with "If anyone thirst,
   let him come to me and drink. . . ." End with "by which
   someone was enabled to bring deliverance." Add sentence
   from page 195 beginning, "The Spirit will teach gently from
   within. . . ."

RESPONSE:
   "You are the breath and the fire," *Your Word Is Near,* p. 107.

SECOND READING:
   Continuation of First Reading, pp. 196–197, the section entitled
   "The Ordinary Gifts of the Spirit," omitting paragraph
   beginning, "It is customary to speak of the seven gifts. . . ."

RESPONSE:
"We pray to you—give us life," p. 108, continuation of response to First Reading.

GOSPEL ACCLAMATION:
"Alleluia! Alleluia," *Biblical Hymns and Psalms*, p. 86.

THE GOSPEL:
John 14:23–27a.

GOSPEL ACCLAMATION:
Repeat from above.

HOMILY

PROFESSION OF FAITH

PERIOD OF REFLECTION:
Intermission

PROCESSIONAL:
"Grant to Us" (Jer. 31:31–34), *Biblical Hymns and Psalms*, p. 40.

PRAYER OF BLESSING OVER GIFTS:
Eucharistic Liturgies, p. 83. May be abbreviated by omitting sentence, "Bless us, Father. . . ."

THE TABLE PRAYER

PREFACE:
"Unity Preface," *The Experimental Liturgy Book*, p. 27.

HYMN OF PRAISE:
"Holy, Holy, Holy," *People's Mass Book*, #106.

ACCLAMATION AT CONSECRATION:
#235a, *People's Mass Book*.

THE SERVICE OF COMMUNION

The "Our Father"

Rite of Peace

Fraction Rite:
Litany of the "Lamb of God"

Song:
"Peace, My Friends," *Come Alive*, p. 30.

Period of Reflection:
Intermission

THE DISMISSAL RITE

Prayer of Benediction:
Eucharistic Liturgies, p. 83.

Blessing and Dismissal

Announcements

Recessional:
"Rejoice, The Lord Is King," *Hymnal for Young Christians*, p. 115.

TRINITY SUNDAY I

Theme: A Celebration of Growth (Appropriate for Graduation Time)

THE ENTRANCE RITE

INVITATION TO WORSHIP:
"Humanity in Progress," Paragraph 20, *Hymn of the Universe,* p. 92.

PROCESSIONAL:
"Priestly People," *People's Mass Book,* #146.

GREETING:
Eucharistic Liturgies, p. 186.

PRAYER OF INVOCATION:
Eucharistic Liturgies, p. 186.

THE SERVICE OF THE WORD

FIRST READING:
Introductory sentence, p. 40, *Faces of Freedom,* followed by excerpt from Vatican Council II, p. 48 of same source.

RESPONSE:
"Grant to Us," *Biblical Hymns and Psalms,* p. 40.

SECOND READING:
Ecclesiasticus 2:1–11(13).

GOSPEL ACCLAMATION:
"Alleluia! Alleluia," *Biblical Hymns and Psalms,* p. 86.

THE GOSPEL:
Luke 6:36–38.

GOSPEL ACCLAMATION:
Repeat from above.

HOMILY

PROFESSION OF FAITH

GENERAL INTENTIONS:
   (*Response:* Lord, hear our prayer.)
   That we may always seek new knowledge and correspond
      with God's grace in learning spiritual and temporal truths,
      we pray to the Lord:
   In thanksgiving for the support and sacrifices that our parents
      have made during the years of our education, we pray to
      the Lord:
   For our teachers who have striven with so much love, effort,
      and patience to give us a good foundation for our future
      learning, we pray to the Lord:
   For our priests that God will reward them for their example
      and service given to us while here at (*name of parish*),
      we pray to the Lord:

PERIOD OF REFLECTION:
   Intermission

PROCESSIONAL:
   "Of My Hands," *Hymnal for Young Christians,* p. 79.

PRAYER OF BLESSING OVER GIFTS:
   Excerpted from *Eucharistic Liturgies,* p. 187. Begin with the
   address, "Father"; continue with "we offer bread and wine:
   the bread of our work. . . ."

THE TABLE PRAYER

PREFACE:
   "Unity Preface," *The Experimental Liturgy Book,* p. 27.

HYMN OF PRAISE:
   "Holy, Holy, Holy! Lord God Almighty," third verse, *People's
   Mass Book,* #184.

ACCLAMATION AT CONSECRATION:
#235a, *People's Mass Book.*

THE SERVICE OF COMMUNION

THE "OUR FATHER"

RITE OF PEACE

FRACTION RITE:
Litany of the "Lamb of God"

SONG:
"My Shepherd Is the Lord" (Ps. 22), *Twenty-Four Psalms and a Canticle,* p. 10.

PERIOD OF REFLECTION:
Intermission

THE DISMISSAL RITE

PRAYER OF BENEDICTION:
Eucharistic Liturgies, p. 187.

BLESSING AND DISMISSAL

ANNOUNCEMENTS

SONG:
"Sing Praise to Our Creator," *People's Mass Book,* #43.

SECOND SUNDAY AFTER PENTECOST I

Theme: A Celebration of Human Freedom in Memory of Those
Who Have Died for It: An Observance of Memorial Day.

THE ENTRANCE RITE

INVITATION TO WORSHIP:
We begin our celebration of human freedom with these words
of Thomas Jefferson: "We hold these truths to be self-evident,
that all men are created equal; that they are endowed by
their Creator with certain inalienable rights; that among these
are life, liberty, and the pursuit of happiness. . . . We mutually
pledge to each other our lives, our fortunes, and our sacred
honor. . . . Error of opinion may be tolerated where reason
is left free to combat it."

PROCESSIONAL:
"My Country 'Tis of Thee."

GREETING:
Eucharistic Liturgies, p. 184.

PRAYER OF INVOCATION:
Excerpted from *Eucharistic Liturgies*, p. 190. Begin with
"Prayer over the Gifts," first two sentences; continue with
"Prayer of the Day," beginning with "If in war . . ." to the end.

THE SERVICE OF THE WORD

FIRST READING:
Ps. 137:1–6.

RESPONSE:
George P. Counts in *Faces of Freedom*, p. 26.

SECOND READING:
Pope John XXIII in *Faces of Freedom*, p. 152.

GOSPEL ACCLAMATION:
"Alleluia! Alleluia!" with first verse, *Biblical Hymns and Psalms,* p. 86.

THE GOSPEL:
Matthew 5:2–10, 38–48.

GOSPEL ACCLAMATION:
Repeat from above, using second verse.

HOMILY

GENERAL INTENTIONS:
(*Response:* Our Father, God of peace, hear our prayer.)
For those who have given their lives for the sake of peace
   and freedom for all mankind, especially for us in America,
   let us pray to the Lord:
For mothers and fathers who have given their children an
   appreciation of freedom and brotherly concern, and
   especially for those parents who have been asked to
   surrender their children for the sake of peace and freedom,
   let us pray to the Lord:
For the people of America and the world, especially our
   leaders, that all may seek ever more fervently new methods
   of arriving at and living in peace, let us pray to the Lord:
In union with our Holy Father, Pope Paul, who pleads, "War,
   war no more, never again war," we ask simply for peace;
   let us pray to the Lord:

PERIOD OF REFLECTION:
Intermission

PROCESSIONAL:
"America, the Beautiful."

PRAYER OF BLESSING OVER GIFTS:
Take these gifts, Father, and bless them, as you blessed the
   offering of your Son, Jesus, who offered his life that others
   might live.

May your grace be with us and all men, now and forever.

THE TABLE PRAYER

PREFACE:
"Eucharistic Prayer by Anne C. Kenney," *The Experimental Liturgy Book*, p. 93. Use first 14 lines, adding, "With all creation we sing your praise."

HYMN OF PRAISE:
"Praise God, From Whom All Blessings Flow," *People's Mass Book*, #45.

ACCLAMATION AT CONSECRATION:
#235a, *People's Mass Book*.

THE SERVICE OF COMMUNION

THE "OUR FATHER"

RITE OF PEACE

FRACTION RITE:
Litany of the "Lamb of God"

SONG:
"Where Charity and Love Prevail," *People's Mass Book*, #121.

PERIOD OF REFLECTION:
Intermission

THE DISMISSAL RITE

PRAYER OF BENEDICTION:
Blessed are you, God our Father, for you have stood by us
   in our darkest hours.
Even when we doubted, you were ever near.

And you have given to mankind that victory which is beyond all others, victory over death itself.

We thank you, Father, for these and all your gifts.

May you be blessed and praised by all men, now and forever.

BLESSING AND DISMISSAL

ANNOUNCEMENTS

RECESSIONAL:
"God Bless America."

THIRD SUNDAY AFTER PENTECOST I

Theme: A Celebration of Man's Hope

THE ENTRANCE RITE

INVITATION TO WORSHIP:
> Our celebration of the Eucharist today focuses upon man's
> hopes for life—its richness of experience, the depth of
> knowledge it can bring, the purpose toward which all life
> tends. We begin our celebration with a reading by Eric Hoffer
> in *Horizons of Hope*, p. 13.

PROCESSIONAL:
> "Hear, O Lord," *Hymnal for Young Christians*, p. 78.

GREETING:
> *Eucharistic Liturgies*, p. 89.

PRAYER OF INVOCATION:
> "Do not turn from us," *Your Word Is Near*, p. 18. Introduce
> with, "Filled with the confidence of the Spirit within us, let
> us pray." End with, "We ask this in the name of Jesus, your
> Son, who with you and the Holy Spirit lives as God, forever
> and ever."

THE SERVICE OF THE WORD

FIRST READING:
> Johannes B. Metz in *Horizons of Hope*, p. 192.

RESPONSE:
> Job 11:16–19 in *Horizons of Hope*, p. 190.

SECOND READING:
> Romans 4:18–25.

GOSPEL ACCLAMATION:
> "Grant to Us," *Biblical Hymns and Psalms*, p. 40.

115

THE GOSPEL:
Luke 7:11–17.

GOSPEL ACCLAMATION:
Repeat from above.

HOMILY

PROFESSION OF FAITH

GENERAL INTENTIONS:
(*Response:* O Lord, our hope, hear our prayer.)
Selection from p. 37, *Your Word Is Near.* Last intention as
follows: For ourselves, that we may keep the words of the
Lord in our hearts and respond to them, finding in that
response our peace and hope, we pray to the Lord:

PERIOD OF REFLECTION:
Intermission

PROCESSIONAL:
"Of My Hands," *Hymnal for Young Christians,* p. 79.

PRAYER OF BLESSING OVER GIFTS:
Father, we gather around this table with hope and confidence.
We come with gifts of bread and wine, knowing that you will
    not turn us away.
We offer you these gifts as signs of our lives together with
    the gift of your Son's life.
All glory be to you, Father, now and forever.
(Adapted from *Eucharistic Liturgies,* p. 90)

THE TABLE PRAYER

PREFACE:
"Canon of Christian Hope," *The Experimental Liturgy Book,*
p. 71.

HYMN OF PRAISE:
"Holy, Holy, Holy! Lord God Almighty," *People's Mass Book,*
#184.

ACCLAMATION AT CONSECRATION:
   "Keep In Mind," *Biblical Hymns and Psalms,* p. 29.

THE SERVICE OF COMMUNION

THE "OUR FATHER"

RITE OF PEACE

FRACTION RITE:
   Litany of the "Lamb of God"

SONG:
   "Whatsoever You Do," *People's Mass Book,* #208.

PERIOD OF REFLECTION:
   Intermission

THE DISMISSAL RITE

PRAYER OF BENEDICTION:
   "We thank you, God, our grace," *Your Word Is Near,* p. 34.
   End with, "This we ask in Jesus' name, who with you and
   the Holy Spirit, lives as God, forever and ever."

BLESSING AND DISMISSAL

ANNOUNCEMENTS

SONG:
   "A Mighty Fortress Is Our God," *People's Mass Book,* #187.

FOURTH SUNDAY AFTER PENTECOST I

Theme: A Celebration of Priestliness

THE ENTRANCE RITE

PROCESSIONAL:
  "Priestly People," *People's Mass Book,* #146.

GREETING:
  Peace to you and blessings from God our Father who has chosen us as his own and has taken his place among us through the work of his Son.

PRAYER OF INVOCATION:
  Rejoicing in the goodness of this world which the Lord has given us, let us pray:
  Father, you have made us people with feelings.
  As men of earth,
     we experience ecstasy and misery,
     finding both boredom and delight
     in ourselves and others.
  Yet you have placed your Word on our shoulders
     and called us to be who we are,
     a people who are in priestly service
     to our world.
  We pray, Father, that we may search
     more carefully and with greater stamina
     for more ways to waken others
     to care for you and live with joy
     for everything that is good and human.
  We ask this through your Son, Christ Jesus,
     who lives together with the Holy Spirit,
     forever and ever.
  (First lines adapted from "You did not make us angels," *Your Word Is Near,* p. 85.)

THE SERVICE OF THE WORD

FIRST READING:
   Exodus 19:2–6a.

RESPONSE:
   "How Can I Repay the Lord" (Antiphon I), *Twenty-Four Psalms and a Canticle*, p. 36.

SECOND READING:
   Section II, #10, *The Constitution on the Church*, pp. 80–83. Omit last 2 sentences of first paragraph.

GOSPEL ACCLAMATION:
   "Alleluia! Alleluia," *Biblical Hymns and Psalms*, p. 86.

THE GOSPEL:
   Matthew 9:36—10:8.

GOSPEL ACCLAMATION:
   Repeat from above.

HOMILY

GENERAL INTENTIONS:
   (*Response:* Lord, hear our prayer.)
   For the courage to know God's Word, and to be able to
      count ourselves among the list of Apostles, regardless of
      the cost, let us pray to the Lord:
   For those who are discouraged and those who make confusion
      an excuse from the demands of the Gospel, let us pray to
      the Lord:
   For those who have gone before us and now rest in the sleep
      of Christ, let us pray to the Lord:
   For bishops and priests, especially those who are exhausted
      and discouraged and find little hope in a people who
      sometimes show little faith, let us pray to the Lord:

PERIOD OF REFLECTION:
   Intermission

PROCESSIONAL:
　　"We Gather Together," *People's Mass Book*, #53.

PRAYER OF BLESSING OVER GIFTS:
　　Eucharistic Liturgies, p. 92.

THE TABLE PRAYER

PREFACE:
　　Gathered around your table, Father,
　　　　we give you thanks for life and love,
　　　　for the bread shared in unity by your children,
　　　　for the wine of gladness—
　　　　for bread and wine in the hands of your Son, Jesus.
　　We thank you for what you have done to your people,
　　　　whom you wish to be your partner
　　　　in a covenant of love.
　　By pouring out over this world your Spirit of life,
　　　　you have led us from captivity;
　　　　you nourish us with the manna of life
　　　　and consecrate us to be your royal priesthood.
　　By your Spirit you purify us and refine us
　　　　to carry your Good News on our shoulders
　　　　so that these tidings may be borne
　　　　to anyone, anywhere in the world.
　　Once more we await a new beginning from you,
　　　　Lord Father and Lord Spirit;
　　　　and with everything that has breath
　　　　we praise you and proclaim you as wonderful,
　　　　singing together with one voice:

HYMN OF PRAISE:
　　"Now Thank We All Our God," third verse, *People's Mass Book*, #178.

ACCLAMATION AT CONSECRATION:
　　#235a, *People's Mass Book*.

ENDING ACCLAMATION
　　"Praise to the Lord," *People's Mass Book*, #175.

THE SERVICE OF COMMUNION

THE "OUR FATHER"

RITE OF PEACE

FRACTION RITE:
Litany of the "Lamb of God"

SONG:
"How Lovely Is Your Dwelling Place," *Thirty Psalms and Two Canticles*, p. 25.

PERIOD OF REFLECTION:
Intermission

THE DISMISSAL RITE

PRAYER OF BENEDICTION:
Eucharistic Liturgies, p. 92. May be abbreviated by omitting second and third sentences.

BLESSING AND DISMISSAL

ANNOUNCEMENTS

RECESSIONAL:
"Behold Among Men," *Biblical Hymns and Psalms*, p. 36.

FIFTH SUNDAY AFTER PENTECOST I

Theme: Father's Day

THE ENTRANCE RITE

INVITATION TO WORSHIP:

Today the parish family of (*name of parish*) celebrates the
fatherhood of our God who shares his fatherly office with man.
We begin our celebration by listening to the words Robert
Kennedy wrote about his father. This passage was read by
Senator Ted Kennedy at the funeral of his brother, Robert:
"What it really adds up to is love, not love as it is described
with such facility in popular magazines, but the kind of love
that is affection and respect, order and encouragement, and
support. Our awareness of this was an incalculable source of
strength and because real love is something unselfish and
involves sacrifice and giving we could not help but profit
from it."

PROCESSIONAL:

"We Gather Together," *People's Mass Book*, #53.

GREETING:

Let us celebrate the goodness
   of God our Father,
   for he has manifested his love for us
   in the mystery of our own father's love.

PRAYER OF INVOCATION:

Father, we are thankful to you
   for all the many gifts of life
   you have shared with us.
Most especially, today, we offer you
   our prayers of gratitude
   for the beauty of fatherhood.
Assist the fathers of our parish
   that they may ever continue to live

so as to teach us
the ideals of your Son, Jesus.
Grant rest and joy to our fathers
who have served you faithfully
and who have gone before us
in the sign of faith.
All of this we ask in the name
of our Lord Jesus,
who with you and the Holy Spirit
lives as God, forever and ever.

THE SERVICE OF THE WORD

FIRST READING:
Ecclesiasticus 3:1–18.

RESPONSE:
John Gardner in *Horizons of Hope*, p. 49.

SECOND READING:
Omitted today.

GOSPEL ACCLAMATION:
"Alleluia! Alleluia," *Biblical Hymns and Psalms*, p. 86.

THE GOSPEL:
Luke 15:11–32.

GOSPEL ACCLAMATION:
Repeat from above.

HOMILY:
If very effective reader(s) is (are) available, it is suggested
that Chapter 10 from *To Kill A Mockingbird* be used as the
homily. The chapter can be cut to concentrate entirely on
Atticus Finch and his son's relation to him.

GENERAL INTENTIONS:
(*Response:* Father of all, hear our prayer.)

In loving remembrance of our fathers who have died, we
   pray to the Lord:
With gratitude to those who are still with us doing the
   things that only a father can do best, we pray to the Lord:
In thanksgiving to God our Father, for giving us the examples
   of justice, love, gentleness, manliness—all of which we have
   found or hope to find in our fathers—we pray to the Lord:
As we celebrate this meal of love and thanksgiving may we
   truly come to live as the sons and daughters of the one
   whom we call our Father, we pray to the Lord:

PERIOD OF REFLECTION:
   Intermission

PROCESSIONAL:
   "How Can I Repay the Lord" (Antiphon I, Ps. 115),
   Twenty-Four Psalms and a Canticle, p. 36.

PRAYER OF BLESSING OVER GIFTS:
   Father, be pleased with this offering
      of bread and wine
      which is a sign of our lives.
   May the example
      of the fathers of our parish family
      continually remind us
      of our duty as Christians to serve you
      as we care for all men as our brothers.
   This we ask through Jesus Christ, your Son,
      who with you and the Spirit, lives as God,
      forever and ever.

THE TABLE PRAYER

PREFACE:
   First 11 lines from "Canon of Christian Service," *The
   Experimental Liturgy Book*, p. 66. Add the following:
   We honor your creation all about us.
   On this day, we especially offer you our thanks
      as we celebrate Father's Day,

for it is by the loving service
and kindness of fathers
that we know of your own loving kindness for us.
And so, with all those joined already with you
we sing in joy:

HYMN OF PRAISE:
"Holy, Holy, Holy! Lord God Almighty," first verse, *People's Mass Book*, #184.

ACCLAMATION AT CONSECRATION:
#235a, *People's Mass Book*.

ENDING ACCLAMATION:
"You Alone Are Holy," *Biblical Hymns and Psalms*, Vol. II, p. 52.

THE SERVICE OF COMMUNION

THE "OUR FATHER"

RITE OF PEACE

FRACTION RITE:
Litany of the "Lamb of God"

SONG:
"Come and Eat of My Bread" (Antiphon II), *People's Mass Book*, #172.

PERIOD OF REFLECTION:
Intermission

THE DISMISSAL RITE

PRAYER OF BENEDICTION:
Your Word Is Near, p. 104. Add this or similar ending, "We

ask this in the name of Jesus, your Son, who with you and
the Holy Spirit lives as God, forever and ever."

BLESSING AND DISMISSAL

ANNOUNCEMENTS

RECESSIONAL:
"Keep in Mind," *People's Mass Book*, #145.

SIXTH SUNDAY AFTER PENTECOST I

Theme: The Mystery of Water: Sign of Salvation

(At one of the Masses on the day for which this liturgy was prepared, an interesting substitute was made for the Entrance Rite and the Service of the Word given below. The children who usually attended a Word Service of their own at this Mass were asked to come thirty minutes early, at which time the pastor gathered them informally in the sanctuary and began a discussion of "Water."

When the adults arrived, they were invited just to listen. After five or ten minutes' further discussion, the pastor gave each child a paper cup and told him to take it to the sacristy, fill it to overflowing, and bring it back—but "Don't spill any on the carpet!" This last admonition was to impress the children with the preciousness of water. After they brought their cups back with breath-taking care, they were allowed to take a sip so that they could put their cups down more easily.

After a few more minutes' discussion the water was blessed; during the baptism that followed, each child was allowed, after the priest, to pour water over the head of the child being baptized. Then the gifts were prepared and the Table Prayer begun.)

THE ENTRANCE RITE

INVITATION TO WORSHIP:
Genesis 7:17–24; 8:1–3.

PROCESSIONAL:
"How Can I Repay the Lord" (Antiphon I, Ps. 115),
Twenty-Four Psalms and a Canticle, p. 36.

GREETING:
From God our Father who sends rains
    to destroy and to enliven:
    may you have wisdom and strength
    to die like the seed, buried and watered,
    in order to come to new life.

127

PRAYER OF INVOCATION:
> Father, we are proud to call you Father,
>   and to stand with your Son.
> He is your total gift to us;
>   in him you bless us beyond all that we deserve.
> Alone we are like the lifeless sands of the desert,
>   but with him we are watered and washed,
>   and spring to life.
> We give you praise through your Son, Jesus Christ,
>   in whom we live, and love and find our meaning.
> All glory be to you, now and forever.
> (Adapted from *Eucharistic Liturgies*, p. 95.)

THE SERVICE OF THE WORD

FIRST READING:
> Job 38:1, 22–30; 40:1–5.

RESPONSE:
> Ps. 65:9, 10, 11–12a, 12b–13 (*by reader*). "He shall descend
> like the rain on the meadows, like the showers that water
> the earth" (*by people—alternated with verses from Ps. 65,
> above*).

SECOND READING:
> Omitted today.

GOSPEL ACCLAMATION:
> "Alleluia! The Strife Is O'er," first verse, *People's Mass Book*,
> #34.

THE GOSPEL:
> Mark 4:35–41.

GOSPEL ACCLAMATION:
> Same as above, third verse.

HOMILY

GENERAL INTENTIONS:

(*Response:* Lord, hear our prayer.)

For perseverence in faith, that fear and panic will not overtake us, that good sense and reason will be our tools along with faith and hope as we fashion the kingdom of God in the image of his Son, let us pray to the Lord:

That we may never be satisfied with anything less than a perfect representation of God's kingdom as we find it in the Gospel, let us pray to the Lord:

That the saving word of God will water us like the spring rains that we might each become fruitful and alive with the spirit of his message to us, let us pray to the Lord:

That those who have become parched and dry, those who are tough and unresponsive, might be softened and humanized by the life-giving breath of God's Spirit in the Church, let us pray to the Lord:

PERIOD OF REFLECTION:

Intermission

PROCESSIONAL:

"Praise the Lord of Heaven," *People's Mass Book,* #180.

PRAYER OF BLESSING OVER GIFTS:

Father, by your goodness
    may these gifts be brought to life;
    may this transformation then bring us to life
    and change us that we might put on
    the attitudes of Christ Jesus your Son.
We ask this in his name,
    who lives with the Holy Spirit
    as God forever and ever.

THE TABLE PRAYER

PREFACE:

Faithful Father, everlasting God,
    we speak and respeak your praises.
In your Spirit you hovered over the waters,

and then penetrated them
   so that they would give life.
By the deluge of rain,
   you hinted at the marvelous way
   in which your love-life would become
   a torrent upon the earth.
And within your people, the Church,
   you have never ceased making love
   by your acts of regeneration
   in the waters of baptism.
We praise you for continually
   sending your Son among us
   as the spring rains that water the earth.
And so with everything that is alive and moving
   because of your loving kindness,
   we praise you, singing together:

HYMN OF PRAISE:
   "Holy, Holy, Holy! Lord God Almighty," third verse, *People's Mass Book*, #184.

ACCLAMATION AT CONSECRATION:
   #235a, *People's Mass Book.*

ENDING ACCLAMATION:
   "You Alone Are Holy," *Biblical Hymns and Psalms*, Vol. II, p. 52.

THE SERVICE OF COMMUNION

THE "OUR FATHER"

RITE OF PEACE

FRACTION RITE:
   Liturgy of the "Lamb of God"

SONG:
   "Come and Eat of My Bread" (Antiphon II), *People's Mass Book*, #172.

PERIOD OF REFLECTION:
   Intermission

THE DISMISSAL RITE

PRAYER OF BENEDICTION:
   Eucharistic Liturgies, p. 96. Omit third and fourth sentences.

BLESSING AND DISMISSAL

ANNOUNCEMENTS

RECESSIONAL:
   "Let Me Sing of Your Law," *Biblical Hymns and Psalms,*
   Vol. II, p. 70.

SEVENTH SUNDAY AFTER PENTECOST I

Theme: The Meaning of Freedom: An Observance of
Independence Day

THE ENTRANCE RITE

INVITATION TO WORSHIP:
The July 4th weekend is the nation's celebration of its
revolution and its independence from Great Britain. In a
special way, we, the people of God, gather to give thanks
and remember the real meaning of freedom and independence
from God's viewpoint, not simply our own. One of our leaders
has reminded us that freedom means that a man stands for
an idea or acts to improve the lot of others or strikes out
against injustice; he sends forth a tiny ripple of hope that
with other ripples can build a current that sweeps down the
mightiest walls of oppression and resistance. All of us will
ultimately be judged and we will surely judge ourselves on
the effort we have contributed to the building of a new
world society and on the extent to which our ideals and goals
have shaped that event.

PROCESSIONAL:
"How Can I Repay the Lord" (Antiphon I, Ps. 115),
Twenty-Four Psalms and a Canticle, p. 36.

GREETING:
Blessings to you and peace
from God our Father
who by his own Son has set us free.

PRAYER OF INVOCATION:
Almighty Father, we praise you and give you thanks
for your gift of self by your Son Jesus.
It was through him that you taught us
how to be free, free from selfishness.
By your Word, speak to us again

132

of the freedom we need
  in order to be your children.
Help us to bear the heavy burden
  of freedom and independence
  and to realize that such things
  are only possible for a people
  who are in unity under your Son's name.
We ask this through Jesus Christ your Son,
  who lives together with the Holy Spirit,
  forever and ever.

THE SERVICE OF THE WORD

FIRST READING:
  Exodus 12:25–27.

COMMENTARY:
  In imitation of the Passover Rite in which the Hebrews
  celebrated their independence from Egypt, we might take
  the same questions they asked about the meaning of their
  celebration and put them in our own terms: Why is this day
  different from all other days? Why do we not work? Why do
  we hear loud voices and see colorful sights on this day? The
  reason? Because we celebrate today a great thing our fathers
  did in this nation. When we were a colony, they revolted and
  rebelled. They said they had a right to rule themselves. They
  wrote this down:
  (Read the "Declaration of Independence.")

RESPONSE:
  "Litany of the Desolate Nation," *Discovery in Prayer*, pp.
  97–99.

SECOND READING:
  Zephaniah 2:1–3.

GOSPEL ACCLAMATION:
  "Alleluia, Alleluia, Alleluia!" (Ps. 150), *People's Mass Book*,
  #163.

THE GOSPEL:
  Luke 4:16–21.

GOSPEL ACCLAMATION:
  Repeat from above.

HOMILY

GENERAL INTENTIONS:
  (*Response:* Lord, hear our prayer.)
  Selection from p. 51, *Your Word Is Near.*

PERIOD OF REFLECTION:
  Intermission

PROCESSIONAL:
  "Let Me Sing of Your Law," *Biblical Hymns and Psalms,*
  Vol. II, p. 70.

PRAYER OF BLESSING OVER GIFTS:
  Father, the gifts we offer at this Mass,
    bread and wine,
    although hardly impressive in themselves,
    are acceptable to you
    because offered by men of faith,
    by men who are free.
  Receive these offerings
    in the name of Christ your Son,
    through whom we give you thanks,
    now and forever.

THE TABLE PRAYER

PREFACE:
  Begin with first fifteen lines of "The Canon of the Pilgrim
  Church," *The Experimental Liturgy Book,* p. 73. Add the
  following:
  In praising you, Lord our God,
    we remember that you have called us

to make this world fit for all to live in;
    you call us to bring good news to the poor,
    sight to the blind.
We remember that you constantly prod us
    to open our minds and hearts to all people,
    to put on the attitude of your Son
    so that we can grow in courage over fear
    and in an appetite for adventure over a love of ease.
And so, with all your creation, we praise you,
    singing together with one voice:

HYMN OF PRAISE:
    "Praise the Lord of Heaven," *Our Parish Prays and Sings*, #13.

ACCLAMATION AT CONSECRATION:
    #235a, *People's Mass Book*.

ENDING ACCLAMATION:
    "You Alone Are Holy," *Biblical Hymns and Psalms*, Vol. II,
    p. 52.

THE SERVICE OF COMMUNION

THE "OUR FATHER"

RITE OF PEACE

FRACTION RITE:
    Liturgy of the "Lamb of God"

SONG:
    "Come and Eat of My Bread" (Antiphon II), *People's Mass Book*, #172.

PERIOD OF REFLECTION:
    Intermission

THE DISMISSAL RITE

PRAYER OF BENEDICTION:
 Blessed are you, God our Father,
  for creating us free.
 You refused to overwhelm us with your power;
  instead you have invited us with your love.
 Our prayer is
  that we may prove worthy of this invitation,
  that we may prove to be men responsible enough
  to use freedom for others,
  and to the glory of your name.
 May you be blessed and praised by all men,
  now and forever.

BLESSING AND DISMISSAL

ANNOUNCEMENTS

RECESSIONAL:
 "Rejoice, the Lord Is King," *Hymnal for Young Christians,*
 p. 115.

EIGHTH SUNDAY AFTER PENTECOST I

Theme: Jesus the Prophet

THE ENTRANCE RITE

INVITATION TO WORSHIP:
Reader invites all to set the theme for today's celebration by
reading together (from their programs) from the first chapter
of Paul's letter to the Ephesians (1:3–14).

PROCESSIONAL:
"Priestly People," *People's Mass Book*, #146.

GREETING:
Wisdom and strength to you,
    prophetic people of God,
    from God our Father,
    and from Jesus Christ his Son,
    whose Spirit moves freely among us,
    calling us forward to hear his good news.
(Adapted from *Eucharistic Liturgies*, p. 99.)

PRAYER OF INVOCATION:
Eucharistic Liturgies, p. 99.

THE SERVICE OF THE WORD

FIRST READING:
Amos 7:12–16a.

RESPONSE:
Matthew 10:17–20.

SECOND READING:
Omitted today.

GOSPEL ACCLAMATION:
"Alleluia! Alleluia," *Biblical Hymns and Psalms*, p. 86.

THE GOSPEL:
Mark 6:1–6.

GOSPEL ACCLAMATION:
Repeat from above.

HOMILY

GENERAL INTENTIONS:
(*Response:* Lord, hear our prayer.)
For those who attempt to live the Gospel, but then find the
price means ridicule and suffering, let us pray to the Lord:
That the Spirit of the Lord of life will help us to put aside
the fears we have of being made new, let us pray to the
Lord:
(For other intentions, make appropriate selection from *Your
Word Is Near*, p. 142.)

PERIOD OF REFLECTION:
Intermission

PROCESSIONAL:
"Come and Eat of My Bread" (Antiphon II), *People's Mass
Book*, #172.

PRAYER OF BLESSING OVER GIFTS:
Eucharistic Liturgies, p. 100. Omit third sentence.

THE TABLE PRAYER

PREFACE:
First and fifth stanzas from "Canon of the Word of God,"
The Experimental Liturgy Book, p. 84.

HYMN OF PRAISE:
"Sing Praise to Our Creator," third verse, *People's Mass Book*,
#43.

ACCLAMATION AT CONSECRATION:
#235a, *People's Mass Book.*

ENDING ACCLAMATION:
"You Alone Are Holy," *Biblical Hymns and Psalms*, Vol. II,
p. 52.

THE SERVICE OF COMMUNION

THE "OUR FATHER"

RITE OF PEACE

FRACTION RITE:
Litany of the "Lamb of God"

SONG:
"At the Lamb's High Feast We Sing," *Our Parish Prays and
Sings*, #2.

PERIOD OF REFLECTION:
Intermission

THE DISMISSAL RITE

PRAYER OF BENEDICTION:
Eucharistic Liturgies, p. 100.

BLESSING AND DISMISSAL

ANNOUNCEMENTS

RECESSIONAL:
"Let Me Sing of Your Law," *Biblical Hymns and Psalms*,
Vol. II, p. 70.

NINTH SUNDAY AFTER PENTECOST I

Theme: The Unity of Christian Action

THE ENTRANCE RITE

INVITATION TO WORSHIP:
> *(by reader and people, as indicated)*

Reader: The people of God believe they are led by the Spirit
of the Lord, who fills the earth. Motivated by this faith, they
labor to decipher authentic signs of God's presence and
purpose in the happenings, needs and desires which they share
with other men of our age. For faith throws a new light on
everything, manifests God's design for man's total vocation,
and thus directs the mind to solutions which are fully human.
We sense that we are a people on the march, that we have
broken the spell of tradition improperly understood—
uncompromising adherence to immovable attitudes, in contrast
with the simplicity, flexibility and dynamism of the Gospel.
In a few years, practically from Pius XII to Paul VI, we have
covered the ground of several centuries on some fundamental
issues. Let us simply think of the following: the eager and
hopeful striving for the union of all Christians, not only to end
the scandal that our division causes, but to fulfill one of
Christ's dearest and most urgent prayers on the eve of his
supreme Sacrifice: That All May Be One; the gradual and
difficult process of bringing about, in the face of all obstacles,
the active participation of the laymen in the common mission
of the Church; the dialogue of the Church with the world,
her opening out to all legitimate values of civilization, and
her search for new "language" forms through which the lasting
message of Christ may reach the hearts of all men.

People: It is true that at times our feet are sore and our hearts
are heavy as we go on our way, because we stumble often
on the stones, because we find thorns among the flowers. All
this simply proves that we are not standing still, that we are
marching toward the future. We have the living certainty
that God's people are going forward, must go forward at the

head of the enormous caravan of men. Only this faith,
pierced through with hope and full of love, can save us,
individually and collectively.
(The Call to Worship is taken from *God's People on Man's
Journey: Proceedings of the Third World Congress for the
Lay Apostolate*, Vol. I, Foreword and pp. 161–162.)

PROCESSIONAL:
"All the Earth Proclaim the Lord," *People's Mass Book*, #141.

GREETING:
The Lord welcomes us whenever we turn to him;
may he be pleased with us now
and give us his peace.

PRAYER OF INVOCATION:
For the wisdom to see life as it really is, let us pray:
Father you turn sadness into joy
and death into life;
you touch the weak things of earth
and make them strong.
Tear from our eyes all that blinds us
to this life as it really is.
May we see and love and give you praise,
now and forever.

THE SERVICE OF THE WORD

FIRST READING:
Exodus 19:5–8.

RESPONSE:
Ps. 46: 4, 5, 8.

SECOND READING:
Ps. 46:1–6, 8–10.

GOSPEL ACCLAMATION:
"Alleluia! Alleluia," *Biblical Hymns and Psalms*, p. 86.

THE GOSPEL:
    Luke 10:1–12.

GOSPEL ACCLAMATION:
    Repeat from above.

HOMILY

GENERAL INTENTIONS:
    (*Response:* Lord, hear our prayer.)
    The apostolate today is made for men as they are, in the
        surroundings where they are. That this lay apostolate here
        present may realize that they share the destiny of all
        mankind, let us pray to the Lord:
    That Christian lay people, in their commitment to earthly
        tasks, may show forth God's love for the world, let us pray
        to the Lord:
    That we be faithful not only in contact with those who do
        not possess faith but also in our relations with those who
        have too much faith, those who doubt, those who see danger
        lurking everywhere, those who cannot shake the mountains
        of hate and injustice, let us pray to the Lord:

PERIOD OF REFLECTION:
    Intermission

PROCESSIONAL:
    "We Shall Go Up With Joy" (Ps. 121), *Twenty-Four Psalms
    and a Canticle*, p. 42.

PRAYER OF BLESSING OVER GIFTS:
    Open our eyes, Father,
        that we may know the way
        you have shown us to peace.
    Cleanse us from all that is deceitful
        that we may stand before you honestly
        and be recognized as your sons.
    We ask this in the name of Jesus Christ

who is your way to life,
through whom you are blessed and praised
now and forever.

THE TABLE PRAYER

PREFACE:
"The Canon of the Pilgrim Church," *The Experimental Liturgy Book*, p. 73.

HYMN OF PRAISE:
"Praise God, From Whom All Blessings Flow," *People's Mass Book*, #45.

ACCLAMATION AT CONSECRATION:
#235a, *People's Mass Book.*

ENDING ACCLAMATION:
"You Alone Are Holy," *Biblical Hymns and Psalms*, Vol. II, p. 52.

THE SERVICE OF COMMUNION

THE "OUR FATHER"

RITE OF PEACE

FRACTION RITE:
Litany of the "Lamb of God"

SONG:
"Come and Eat of My Bread" (Antiphon II), *People's Mass Book*, #172.

PERIOD OF REFLECTION:
Intermission

THE DISMISSAL RITE

PRAYER OF BENEDICTION:
  Eucharistic Liturgies, p. 102.

BLESSING AND DISMISSAL

ANNOUNCEMENTS

RECESSIONAL:
  "Behold Among Men," *Biblical Hymns and Psalms,* p. 36.

TENTH SUNDAY AFTER PENTECOST I

Theme: A Celebration of Each Man's Talent

THE ENTRANCE RITE

INVITATION TO WORSHIP:
Martin Luther King in *Horizons of Hope*, p. 40.

PROCESSIONAL:
"Praise to the Lord," *People's Mass Book*, #175.

GREETING:
The Lord knows what we need
even before we ask him.

PRAYER OF INVOCATION:
Filled with confidence in the love of our Father in heaven,
let us pray:
Father, accept our prayers
and make us receptive
to everything you can give us.
All glory be to you, and to your Son,
and to the Spirit of life,
now and forever.

THE SERVICE OF THE WORD

FIRST READING:
1 Corinthians 12:2–11.

RESPONSE:
Romans 12:6–8.

SECOND READING:
Ps. 146:1–10.

GOSPEL ACCLAMATION:
"Alleluia! Alleluia," *Biblical Hymns and Psalms*, p. 86.

145

THE GOSPEL:
    Luke 11:1–13.

GOSPEL ACCLAMATION:
    Repeat from above.

HOMILY

GENERAL INTENTIONS:
    (*Response:* Lord, hear our prayer.)
    For those who fail to recognize the beauty and uniqueness
        which their individuality can offer to the world in which
        they live, let us pray to the Lord:
    For those who, being so concerned with their own needs,
        fail to recognize the rights and human feelings of those
        closest to them, let us pray to the Lord:
    For peace of mind to those who are insecure; for mercy
        and forgiveness on the part of those offended; for
        compassion and understanding from those who seek such
        consideration, let us pray to the Lord:
    For ourselves, that we would never be unmindful of the
        generosity of our Father and that we would respond to
        his love by the love and service which we offer to others,
        let us pray to the Lord:
    (*Celebrant adds the following:*)
    Take care of your people, Lord, as they journey toward
    you, and listen when they call upon you.

PERIOD OF REFLECTION:
    Intermission

PROCESSIONAL:
    "Of My Hands," *Hymnal for Young Christians,* p. 79.

PRAYER OF BLESSING OVER GIFTS:
    Eucharistic Liturgies, p. 105. Omit third and fourth sentences.

THE TABLE PRAYER

PREFACE:
"Eucharistic Prayer of Human Unity," *The Experimental Liturgy Book,* p. 100.

HYMN OF PRAISE:
"Sing Praise to Our Creator," third verse, *People's Mass Book,* #43.

ACCLAMATION AT CONSECRATION:
#235a, *People's Mass Book.*

ENDING ACCLAMATION:
"You Alone Are Holy," *Biblical Hymns and Psalms,* Vol. II, p. 52.

THE SERVICE OF COMMUNION

THE "OUR FATHER"

RITE OF PEACE

FRACTION RITE:
Litany of the "Lamb of God"

SONG:
"They'll Know We Are Christians by Our Love," *Hymnal for Young Christians,* p. 132.

PERIOD OF REFLECTION:
Intermission

THE DISMISSAL RITE

PRAYER OF BENEDICTION:
Eucharistic Liturgies, p. 105.

BLESSING AND DISMISSAL

ANNOUNCEMENTS

RECESSIONAL:
"To Jesus Christ, Our Sovereign King," *People's Mass Book*,
#48.

ELEVENTH SUNDAY AFTER PENTECOST I

Theme: Faith in Christ—The True Bread from Heaven

THE ENTRANCE RITE

INVITATION TO WORSHIP:
Introduction on p. 128, *Horizons of Hope*. Substitute the
word "faith" for "hope" in the first sentence.

PROCESSIONAL:
"Grant to Us" (Jer. 31:31–34), *Biblical Hymns and Psalms*,
p. 40.

GREETING:
Eucharistic Liturgies, p. 107.

PRAYER OF INVOCATION:
Eucharistic Liturgies, p. 107.

THE SERVICE OF THE WORD

FIRST READING:
Isaiah 40:28–31.

RESPONSE:
"You, God, arouse faith in our hearts," *Your Word Is Near*,
p. 17.

SECOND READING:
Ps. 78:3–8.

GOSPEL ACCLAMATION:
"Alleluia, Alleluia, Alleluia," *People's Mass Book*, #163.

THE GOSPEL:
John 6:22–35.

GOSPEL ACCLAMATION:
Repeat from above.

HOMILY

GENERAL INTENTIONS:
(*Response:* Lord, let our faith be true.)
That those in public office will be guided by truth,
   let us pray to the Lord:
For the sick and the poor, that they might not lose faith
   and hope in themselves, let us pray to the Lord:
For those suffering from disillusionment at the sight of the
   world today; for those who want sincerely to believe but
   cannot; for those who seek for nothing to hope in, yet
   search daily for meaning in their lives, let us pray to
   the Lord:
For those who teach us of the love of God for us, his people,
   that they may always speak the truth as they know it in
   their hearts and for those who listen to them, let us pray
   to the Lord:
For all of us here that we will always remain nourished
   with the bread from heaven which gives life to the world,
   let us pray to the Lord:

PERIOD OF REFLECTION:
Intermission

PROCESSIONAL:
"Come and Eat of My Bread" (Antiphon II), *People's Mass
Book,* #172.

PRAYER OF BLESSING OVER GIFTS:
Father, we set before you simple gifts of bread and
   wine, knowing that without your love and power,
   they will be as nothing.
And yet as we present these gifts
   we profess to believe
   that you can give them new meaning and worth
   just as you can give meaning and worth to our lives.

Be pleased with this offering and our act of faith,
   and by these gifts transform our lives.
We ask and hope for this
   in the name of Jesus, your Son,
    who with you and the Spirit lives forever and ever.

THE TABLE PRAYER

PREFACE:
   "The Canon of Christian Hope," *The Experimental Liturgy Book*, p. 71.

HYMN OF PRAISE:
   "Holy, Holy, Holy, Lord God Almighty," *People's Mass Book*, #184.

ACCLAMATION AT CONSECRATION:
   #235a, *People's Mass Book*.

ENDING ACCLAMATION:
   "Praise to the Lord," third verse, *People's Mass Book*, #175.

THE SERVICE OF COMMUNION

THE "OUR FATHER"

RITE OF PEACE

FRACTION RITE:
   Liturgy of the "Lamb of God"

SONG:
   "God Is Love," *Hymnal for Young Christians*, p. 95.

PERIOD OF REFLECTION:
   Intermission

THE DISMISSAL RITE

PRAYER OF BENEDICTION:
 Father, we thank you for your goodness
  which you constantly manifest toward us,
   your chosen sons and daughters.
 May we be ever mindful of the words
  which your Son, Jesus, has spoken to us this day,
   and your own words.
 By the strength of this Eucharist may we have the courage
  to live and to bring to others
   the joy and wonder of life and its many beauties.
 This we ask in the name of your Son, Jesus, our Lord,
  who with you and the Holy Spirit,
   lives forever and ever.

BLESSING AND DISMISSAL

ANNOUNCEMENTS

RECESSIONAL:
 "Now Thank We All Our God," *People's Mass Book,* #178.

TWELFTH SUNDAY AFTER PENTECOST I

Theme: Hope Is Seeing God in the Here and Now

THE ENTRANCE RITE

INVITATION TO WORSHIP:
George Santanyana, in *Listen to Love*, p. 303.

PROCESSIONAL:
"Yes I Shall Arise," *People's Mass Book*, #147.

GREETING:
Eucharistic Liturgies, p. 110.

PRAYER OF INVOCATION:
Eucharistic Liturgies, p. 110.

THE SERVICE OF THE WORD

FIRST READING:
Colossians 3:1–5, 9–11.

RESPONSE:
Ps. 40:1, 2, 3, 17 (*by reader*).
"Lord, come to my aid" (*by people—alternated with verses from Ps. 40, above*).

SECOND READING:
Omitted today.

GOSPEL ACCLAMATION:
"Sing Praise to the Lord," *People's Mass Book*, #202.

THE GOSPEL:
Luke 12:13–21.

GOSPEL ACCLAMATION:
Repeat from above.

HOMILY

GENERAL INTENTIONS:
   (*Response:* Increase our trust in you, O Lord.)
   First two paragraphs, p. 37, *Your Word Is Near.*

PERIOD OF REFLECTION:
   Intermission

PROCESSIONAL:
   "Priestly People," *People's Mass Book,* #146.

PRAYER OF BLESSING OVER GIFTS:
   Eucharistic Liturgies, p. 111.

THE TABLE PRAYER

PREFACE:
   "The Canon of Christian Hope," *The Experimental Liturgy
   Book,* p. 71.

HYMN OF PRAISE:
   "Praise the Lord of Heaven," *Our Parish Prays and Sings,* #13.

ACCLAMATION AT CONSECRATION:
   "Keep in Mind," *People's Mass Book,* #145.

ENDING ACCLAMATION:
   "You Alone Are Holy," *Biblical Hymns and Psalms,* Vol. II,
   p. 52.

THE SERVICE OF COMMUNION

THE "OUR FATHER"

RITE OF PEACE

FRACTION RITE:
   Litany of the "Lamb of God"

SONG:
"Without Seeing You," *People's Mass Book,* #173.

PERIOD OF REFLECTION:
Intermission

THE DISMISSAL RITE

PRAYER OF BENEDICTION:
Eucharistic Liturgies, p. 108.

BLESSING AND DISMISSAL

ANNOUNCEMENTS

RECESSIONAL:
"Sent Forth by God's Blessing," *People's Mass Book,* #138.

THIRTEENTH SUNDAY AFTER PENTECOST I

Theme: A Celebration of the Church Visible

THE ENTRANCE RITE

INVITATION TO WORSHIP:
   Karl Barth in *Listen to Love*, p. 257.

PROCESSIONAL:
   "We Gather Together," *People's Mass Book*, #53.

GREETING:
   Eucharistic Liturgies, p. 112.

PRAYER OF INVOCATION:
   Mindful that we who stand before God our Father are
      incomplete and death-bound until we are one with his
      Son, let us pray:
   Father, the work of your Son is still incomplete,
      and we struggle with him
      to bring it to fulfillment.
   Only when we have built here
      a city of peace and love
      will you be pleased to dwell with us
      in a life that will never end.
   Bread and wine, Body and Blood, give us the strength
      to live the tension and ambiguity
      that is our lot
      in peace and confidence and hope.
   We bless your name in all that we do and say
      now and forever.
   (Excerpted and adapted from *Eucharistic Liturgies*, p. 115.)

THE SERVICE OF THE WORD

FIRST READING:
   Proverbs 9:1–6.

RESPONSE:
"O Taste and See the Goodness of the Lord," *Psalms for Singing*, Book One, p. 14.

SECOND READING:
Ephesians 5:15–20.

RESPONSE:
A few minutes of silent reflection.

GOSPEL ACCLAMATION:
"Alleluia! Alleluia," *People's Mass Book*, #167.

THE GOSPEL:
John 5:51–58.

GOSPEL ACCLAMATION:
Repeat from above.

HOMILY

GENERAL INTENTIONS:
(*Response:* Lord, hear our prayer.)
Second paragraph, p. 125, *Your Word Is Near*.

PERIOD OF REFLECTION:
Intermission

PROCESSIONAL:
"Come and Eat of My Bread" (Antiphon II), *People's Mass Book*, #172.

PRAYER OF BLESSING OVER GIFTS:
Let us pray that my sacrifice and yours will be acceptable
to God our Almighty Father:
This bread and this wine are taken from the earth
and given to you, Father—
simple gifts, yet gifts to speak our love for you.

We ask you to make them new,
   and through them to make us new,
      that we may be the Body of your Son here on earth.
Through him we give you praise today and every day,
   forever and ever.

THE TABLE PRAYER

PREFACE:
   "Canon of the New Creation," *Eucharistic Liturgies*, p. 208.

HYMN OF PRAISE:
   "Praise to the Lord," *People's Mass Book*, p. 261.

ACCLAMATION AT CONSECRATION:
   #235a, *People's Mass Book*.

ENDING ACCLAMATION:
   "You Alone Are Holy," *Biblical Hymns and Psalms*, Vol. II,
   p. 52.

THE SERVICE OF COMMUNION

THE "OUR FATHER"

RITE OF PEACE

FRACTION RITE:
   Litany of the "Lamb of God"

SONG:
   Omitted today.

PERIOD OF REFLECTION:
   Intermission

THE DISMISSAL RITE

PRAYER OF BENEDICTION:
"We have heard your word, O God," *Your Word Is Near,* p. 123.

BLESSING AND DISMISSAL

ANNOUNCEMENTS

RECESSIONAL:
"All the Earth," *People's Mass Book,* #141.

FOURTEENTH SUNDAY AFTER PENTECOST I

Theme: A Celebration of the Servant Church

THE ENTRANCE RITE

INVITATION TO WORSHIP:
Last Sunday we considered the role of the Bread of Life,
or the Body of Christ, as formative of the bond of unity and
brotherhood which gives rise to a servant Church. Today we
will try to deepen our understanding of this servant Church
as we listen to the Word of God, first of all, from the book
of Joshua, in which the people of Israel dedicate themselves
to the service of the Lord. Then, in Paul's letter we will
hear a description of the Church as he compares it to
matrimony; and in the Gospel we will continue last week's
reading and reflect upon the mystery of faith as it guides
those who hear and can accept God's Word, Jesus Christ.

PROCESSIONAL:
"At the Lamb's High Feast," *Our Parish Prays and Sings,* #2.

GREETING:
Eucharistic Liturgies, p. 117.

PRAYER OF INVOCATION:
Eucharistic Liturgies, p. 117. Omit second and third sentences.

THE SERVICE OF THE WORD

FIRST READING:
Joshua 24:1–2a ("Then Joshua said to all the people:"); 15–18.

RESPONSE:
"O Taste and See the Goodness of the Lord" (Ps. 33), *Psalms
for Singing,* Book One, p. 14.

SECOND READING:
Ephesians 5:21–32.

GOSPEL ACCLAMATION:
"Alleluia! Alleluia," *Biblical Hymns and Psalms,* p. 86.

THE GOSPEL:
John 6:60–69.

GOSPEL ACCLAMATION:
Repeat from above.

HOMILY

GENERAL INTENTIONS:
(*Response:* Lord, make us one in serving you.)
Selection from pp. 125–126, *Your Word Is Near.*

PERIOD OF REFLECTION:
Intermission

PROCESSIONAL:
"Come and Eat of My Bread" (Antiphon II), *People's Mass Book,* #172.

PRAYER OF BLESSING OVER GIFTS:
Eucharistic Liturgies, p. 118. Use only second and fifth sentences.

THE TABLE PRAYER

PREFACE:
"Canon of Christian Service," *The Experimental Liturgy Book,* p. 66.

HYMN OF PRAISE:
"Holy, Holy, Holy! Lord God Almighty," *People's Mass Book,* #184.

ACCLAMATION AT CONSECRATION:
#235a, *People's Mass Book.*

ENDING ACCLAMATION:
  "You Alone Are Holy," *Biblical Hymns and Psalms*, Vol. II,
  p. 52.

THE SERVICE OF COMMUNION

THE "OUR FATHER"

RITE OF PEACE

FRACTION RITE:
  Litany of the "Lamb of God"

SONG:
  "Look Beyond," *Hymnal for Young Christians*, Vol II, p. 9.

PERIOD OF REFLECTION:
  Intermission

THE DISMISSAL RITE

PRAYER OF BENEDICTION:
  Eucharistic Liturgies, p. 118. Omit second, fourth, and fifth
  sentences.

BLESSING AND DISMISSAL

ANNOUNCEMENTS

RECESSIONAL:
  "Praise God, From Whom All Blessings Flow," *People's Mass
  Book*, #45.

FIFTEENTH SUNDAY AFTER PENTECOST I

Theme: A Celebration of Man in Autumn

THE ENTRANCE RITE

INVITATION TO WORSHIP:
"The Music of the Autumn Winds," *Listen to Love*, p. 270.

PROCESSIONAL:
"The Church's One Foundation," *People's Mass Book*, #223.

GREETING:
May the God of our Fathers,
   who manifests himself in nature and in men,
   continue to allow his face to shine upon you.

PRAYER OF INVOCATION:
"You have made your dwelling," *Your Word Is Near*, p. 139.
Introduce with: "As sons and daughters confident in our
Father's love and concern for us, let us pray:"

THE SERVICE OF THE WORD

FIRST READING:
Ecclesiasticus 3:17(19)–20(21); 28(30)–29(31).

RESPONSE:
Elizabeth Barrett Browning in *Listen to Love*, p. 226; then
a few moments in silent reflection.

SECOND READING:
Hebrews 12:18–19, 22–24a.

GOSPEL ACCLAMATION:
"Alleluia, Alleluia, Alleluia," *People's Mass Book*, #86c.

163

THE GOSPEL:
Luke 14:1, 7–14.

GOSPEL ACCLAMATION:
Repeat from above.

HOMILY

GENERAL INTENTIONS:
(*Response:* Lord, let us see you.)
For all those who are blind to the presence of Christ in our
world; for those who are deaf and insensitive to his needs,
let us pray to the Lord:
For all our fellow men who are in pain and misery; for
those about us who are so busy that they miss the beauty
and the reality of life, let us pray to the Lord:
For those in public office, that they may not tolerate injustice
and greed; for those campaigning for public office, that they
may promise only what they can give; for all citizens,
that they may study the issues and the candidates and vote
for those who can best serve the needs of the people, who
are Christ in the world, let us pray to the Lord:
For ourselves, that, as we share in this bread and wine and
call upon the Lord to be present among us, we may realize
that by our concern for others we are making Christ visible
in the world, let us pray to the Lord:

PERIOD OF REFLECTION:
Intermission

PROCESSIONAL:
"Without Seeing You," *People's Mass Book,* #173.

PRAYER OF BLESSING OVER GIFTS:
Our Father, to you we offer the gifts
of harvested grain and plucked fruit,
our bread and wine, the symbols of our lives.
We come to sit at table with your Son
and to share in his presence by our sharing of this bread.

Bless our assembly and make to happen all that we believe
  by our gathering here in peace.
We ask this in Jesus' name,
  who with you and the Holy Spirit,
  lives as God, forever and ever.

THE TABLE PRAYER

PREFACE:
  "The Canon of Christian Hope," *The Experimental Liturgy
  Book*, p. 71.

HYMN OF PRAISE:
  "O God, Almighty Father," *Our Parish Prays and Sings*, #12.

ACCLAMATION AT CONSECRATION:
  "Keep in Mind," *People's Mass Book*, #145.

ENDING ACCLAMATION:
  "You Alone Are Holy," *Biblical Hymns and Psalms*, Vol. II,
  p. 52.

THE SERVICE OF COMMUNION

THE "OUR FATHER"

RITE OF PEACE

FRACTION RITE:
  Litany of the "Lamb of God"

SONG:
  "My Shepherd Is the Lord" (Ps. 22, Antiphon I), *Twenty-Four
  Psalms and a Canticle*, p. 10.

PERIOD OF REFLECTION:
  Intermission

THE DISMISSAL RITE

PRAYER OF BENEDICTION:
> Father, you have come among us and called us
> > with the voice of your Son, Jesus.
>
> By our trust in his Word and the strength of your holy bread
> > may we be a new people, a new beginning
> > of hope and peace in this wide, uncertain world.
>
> We ask this in the name of Jesus,
> > he who lives with you and the Holy Spirit, as God,
> > forever and ever.

BLESSING AND DISMISSAL

ANNOUNCEMENTS

RECESSIONAL:
> "A Mighty Fortress," *People's Mass Book,* #187.

SIXTEENTH SUNDAY AFTER PENTECOST I

Theme: A Celebration of Work—Man's Sharing In God's Creation

THE ENTRANCE RITE

INVITATION TO WORSHIP:

Work is generally considered a purely material thing,
unrelated to the service of God. This is not so: each of us
must apply Christianity to his occupation. This celebration is
really a celebration of work, of Christ's work, and of our work
in Christ. Work, in God's eyes, is redemptive. Christ gave
effect to this on his Cross, and continues to do so in the
sacrament of our celebration. Our work is one of the ways
by which we express our sharing in the new creation process.
We must try to gain the lively conviction that our daily labor
gives positive support to the "work" Christ did and is still
doing.

PROCESSIONAL:

"They'll Know We Are Christians," third and second verses in
that order, *Hymnal for Young Christians*, p. 132.

GREETING:

May the God of our fathers
  who has worked his wonders among us
  and who each day offers us a new world be with you.

PRAYER OF INVOCATION:

Mindful that our work is not in vain but a real part of making
the world a finished product, let us pray:
Father, you have made us in your own image.
You have placed in our hands a universe rich in resources
  and potential.
You have given us the example of your Son, Jesus.
We pray that we may respond with awareness and sensitivity
  to the possibilities open to us.
We pray that we may cooperate with you,

167

bringing creation to fulfillment.

This we ask in the name of your Son, our Lord Jesus,
who with you and the Holy Spirit, lives as God
forever and ever.

THE SERVICE OF THE WORD

FIRST READING:
Ps. 127.

RESPONSE:
Silent reflection.

SECOND READING:
Colossians 3:23–24.

GOSPEL ACCLAMATION:
"Alleluia! The Strife Is O'er," first verse, *People's Mass Book,*
#34.

THE GOSPEL:
John 6:27–29.

GOSPEL ACCLAMATION:
"Alleluia! The Strife Is O'er," cited above, third verse.

HOMILY

GENERAL INTENTIONS:
(*Response:* Lord, accept us as your workers.)

That Christian workers bring to their labor their witness to a
living faith, let us pray to the Lord:

That the Christians here assembled realize that they can join
the pain of the work of their hands to the sacrifice of
Christ, let us pray to the Lord:

That scientists, engineers and workers everywhere have a
clear vision of their responsibility to work toward a new
creation, let us pray to the Lord:

For all of us, that we realize that by being what we are,

by using the unique talents of our own individuality, we are constantly renewing God's creation, let us pray to the Lord:

PERIOD OF REFLECTION:
Intermission

PROCESSIONAL:
"Grant to Us," *Biblical Hymns and Psalms,* p. 40.

PRAYER OF BLESSING OVER GIFTS:
Father, in the manner of your Son,
and in the power of the Holy Spirit,
we offer you these gifts of bread and wine
as signs of our commitment
to your work of forming the earth.
May all that we do give glory to you, God our Father,
who with the Son and the Spirit, lives and reigns forever.

THE TABLE PRAYER

PREFACE:
"Canon of the New Creation," *The Underground Mass Book,* p. 24.

HYMN OF PRAISE:
"Praise God, From Whom All Blessings Flow," *People's Mass Book,* #45.

ACCLAMATION AT CONSECRATION:
#235a, *People's Mass Book.*

ENDING ACCLAMATION:
"Praise to the Lord," second verse, *People's Mass Book,* #175.

THE SERVICE OF COMMUNION

THE "OUR FATHER"

RITE OF PEACE

FRACTION RITE:
Litany of the "Lamb of God"

SONG:
"We Shall Go Up With Joy" (Ps. 121, Antiphon I),
Twenty-Four Psalms and a Canticle, p. 42.

PERIOD OF REFLECTION:
Intermission

THE DISMISSAL RITE

PRAYER OF BENEDICTION:
Father, look with favor upon this world,
   its nations and cultures,
   homes and schools, arts, commerce and industry,
   the occupations and leisure of all.
Enable us, in however small a way, to improve
   what you have begun on this earth
   through Jesus Christ, your Son, our Lord,
   who lives and rules with you and the Holy Spirit,
   as God, forever and ever.

BLESSING AND DISMISSAL

ANNOUNCEMENTS

RECESSIONAL:
"Crown Him with Many Crowns," *People's Mass Book,* #49.

SEVENTEENTH SUNDAY AFTER PENTECOST I

Theme: A Reflection on Suffering

THE ENTRANCE RITE

INVITATION TO WORSHIP:
>Today, gathered as God's people, we remember that life and love know suffering. Is there an answer to it, especially when endured by the innocent? From the Book of Job we hear this episode:
>Job 2:1–10.

PROCESSIONAL:
>"O Sacred Head, Surrounded," *People's Mass Book*, #27.

GREETING:
>Blessed be God the Father of all consolation,
>>who comforts us in our sufferings
>>so that we in turn may comfort others in theirs.

PRAYER OF INVOCATION:
>"You have given your Son to us," *Your Word Is Near*, p. 58.

THE SERVICE OF THE WORD

FIRST READING:
>Isaiah 50:4–9.

RESPONSE:
>1 Corinthians 1:18, 23–25.

SECOND READING:
>James 2:14–17.

RESPONSE:
>Louis Evely in *Listen to Love*, p. 80.

THE GOSPEL:
>Mark 14:33–35.

Gospel Acclamation:
#190b, *People's Mass Book.*

Homily

General Intentions:
(*Response:* Let it be done unto me according to your will.)
For compassion in the face of others' suffering, let us pray
to the Lord:
In sorrow for attitudes of revenge, let us pray to the Lord:
For faith that lives, and is marked by deeds of service, let
us pray to the Lord:
That we may never become the cause of another's suffering,
let us pray to the Lord:

Period of Reflection:
Intermission

Processional:
"How Can I Repay the Lord" (Ps. 115, Antiphon I),
Twenty-Four Psalms and a Canticle, p. 36.

Prayer of Blessing over Gifts:
Receive, eternal Father, these gifts which we offer together.
Nourished by the broken but risen Body of your Son,
    we accept the life you offer us
    with all its suffering and its joys.
Make us gentle and humble enough
    to help other people and comfort them,
    so that a little of your love may be seen in us.
We ask this through your Son, Jesus,
    who lives with the Spirit, forever and ever.

THE TABLE PRAYER

Preface:
Lord God, Almighty Father, what would our life be
    without you?

To you we owe the peace conquering fear,
    the hope encouraging us, and the love setting us free.
We come together to give thanks
    for being able to know you through your Son, Jesus Christ.
We speak with reverence and in hope of blessing
    the name of Jesus,
    for in the days of his mortal life,
    he bore our frailties, but in his anxieties
    he prayed to you and you heard him.
Because he lived without power or prestige,
    he was killed at the hands of men,
    but you raised him to life,
    giving him a name above all names on this earth.
Confidently we come to you,
    knowing that if we suffer with Christ,
    we will be raised with him.
And so with all creation rising to meet you,
    we sing your praises, singing together:
(Adapted from *Your Word Is Near*, pp. 57 and 63.)

HYMN OF PRAISE:
    "Praise the Lord of Heaven," *People's Mass Book*, #180.

ACCLAMATION AT CONSECRATION:
    #235a, *People's Mass Book.*

ENDING ACCLAMATION:
    "You Alone Are Holy," *Biblical Hymns and Psalms*, Vol. II,
    p. 52.

THE SERVICE OF COMMUNION

THE "OUR FATHER"

RITE OF PEACE

FRACTION RITE:
    Litany of the "Lamb of God"

SONG:
"My Soul Is Thirsting for the Lord" (Ps. 41, Antiphon I),
Twenty-Four Psalms and a Canticle, p. 16.

PERIOD OF REFLECTION:
Intermission

THE DISMISSAL RITE

PRAYER OF BENEDICTION:
"We have your promise, God," *Your Word Is Near*, p. 62.
Use first three sentences, adding to the last, ". . . looking
beyond our own hurt to the understanding and comfort
we can bring to others in their distress."

BLESSING AND DISMISSAL

ANNOUNCEMENTS

RECESSIONAL:
"All Glory, Praise, and Honor," *People's Mass Book*, #29.

EIGHTEENTH SUNDAY AFTER PENTECOST I

Theme: Justice, Order, and Peace

THE ENTRANCE RITE

INVITATION TO WORSHIP:
> The following reading is taken from a political speech.
> Please listen to it carefully, as, together with your response,
> it sets the theme for today's celebration: "The streets of our
> country are in turmoil. The universities are filled with students
> rebelling and rioting. Communists are seeking to destroy our
> country. Russia is threatening us with her might and the
> Republic is in danger. Yes, danger from within and without.
> We need law and order. Yes, without law and order our
> nation cannot survive. Elect us and we shall restore law and
> order." *(After a moment's pause, continue.)* The speech was
> given in 1932 by Adolph Hitler. In 1964 the Church, gathered
> in council, responded to the problems of war and oppression
> by defining the nature of true peace. Let us, who are the
> Church gathered together now, make the same response:
> All read together this passage from paragraph 78 of the
> "Pastoral Constitution on the Church in the Modern World":
> First two sentences; continue with "Peace is never attained
> once and for all . . ." through ". . . which goes beyond what
> love can provide."

PROCESSIONAL:
> "A Mighty Fortress Is Our God," *People's Mass Book*, #187.

GREETING:
> To all who are weary from the struggle of bringing to
>   birth true justice:
> May the grace and peace of God, the loving Father,
>   of Jesus, the sign of his love,
>   and their Spirit which renews the face of the earth,
>   be with you.

PRAYER OF INVOCATION:

> Mindful that we Christian people, the living Christ,
>> must be the way and the light to a searching, tired world,
>> we pray:
> Lord, let us not seek for order at the expense of justice,
>> settling for less than you have offered us.
> Teach us by your Word to walk the path of your Son,
>> thirsting for justice and peace.
> May we never, in our weariness, concede
>> that superficial order will bring
>> what only your Son and his life can establish.
> We ask this in his name now and forever.

THE SERVICE OF THE WORD

FIRST READING:
> Wisdom 2:12, 17–20.

RESPONSE:
> Ps. 54:1–4, 6.

SECOND READING:
> James 3:16–18; 4:1–3.

RESPONSE:
> Margaret Mead in *Faces of Freedom*, p. 190.

GOSPEL ACCLAMATION:
> "Alleluia! The Strife Is O'er," third verse, *People's Mass Book*, #34.

THE GOSPEL:
> Mark 9:30–37.

GOSPEL ACCLAMATION:
> #190b, *People's Mass Book*.

HOMILY

GENERAL INTENTIONS:
(*Response:* O Lord, hear our prayer.)
Selection from pp. 98–99, *Your Word Is Near.*

PERIOD OF REFLECTION:
Intermission

PROCESSIONAL:
"Bring to the Lord Your Offerings" (Ps. 28, Antiphon III),
Twenty-Four Psalms and a Canticle, p. 14.

PRAYER OF BLESSING OVER GIFTS:
Eucharistic Liturgies, p. 125. Omit second, third, and fourth
sentences.

THE TABLE PRAYER

PREFACE:
It is not only right, but helpful, for us
  to give you thanks, Father, at all times and places.
We do so now through Jesus our brother,
  who lived among us full of grace and truth.
He died to destroy death
  and rose that we might live forever with him.
With the Church through all the ages,
  and with all men who have lived and share your life,
  we sing your praise together and say:
(Adapted from the Preface for Easter in *The English-Latin
Sacramentary.*)

HYMN OF PRAISE:
"Praise God, From Whom All Blessings Flow," *People's Mass
Book*, #45.

ACCLAMATION AT CONSECRATION:
#235a, *People's Mass Book.*

ENDING ACCLAMATION:
"You Alone Are Holy," *Biblical Hymns and Psalms*, Vol. II,
p. 52.

THE SERVICE OF COMMUNION

THE "OUR FATHER"

RITE OF PEACE

FRACTION RITE:
Litany of the "Lamb of God"

SONG:
"Peace, My Friends," *Hymnal for Young Christians*, Vol. II, p. 34.

PERIOD OF REFLECTION:
Intermission

THE DISMISSAL RITE

PRAYER OF BENEDICTION:
Eucharistic Liturgies, p. 125.

BLESSING AND DISMISSAL

ANNOUNCEMENTS

RECESSIONAL:
"Sion, Sing," *People's Mass Book*, #165.

NINETEENTH SUNDAY AFTER PENTECOST I

Theme: Conversion

THE ENTRANCE RITE

PROCESSIONAL:
"O God, Our Help In Ages Past," *People's Mass Book,* #185.

GREETING:
Eucharistic Liturgies, p. 126.

PRAYER OF INVOCATION:
Eucharistic Liturgies, p. 126. Omit second and third sentences.

THE SERVICE OF THE WORD

FIRST READING:
Ezekiel 33:10–16.

RESPONSE:
Ps. 25:4–9.

SECOND READING:
Philippians 2:1–11.

RESPONSE:
Silent reflection; then "Alleluia! Alleluia," *Biblical Hymns and Psalms,* p. 86.

THE GOSPEL:
Matthew 21:28–32.

GOSPEL ACCLAMATION:
Repeat from above.

HOMILY

GENERAL INTENTIONS:
(*Response:* Lord, hear our prayer.)

For all those, throughout the world, who believe in the gospel,
that they may grow in grace and humanity, let us pray to
the Lord:

That all of us may continually be converted, receiving the
Spirit of Jesus, our Lord, who is the light and life, hope
and peace of this world, forever and ever, let us pray
to the Lord:

PERIOD OF REFLECTION:
Intermission

PROCESSIONAL:
"At the Name of Jesus," *The Hymnal of the Protestant
Episcopal Church in the United States of America,* #356.

PRAYER OF BLESSING OVER GIFTS:
Eucharistic Liturgies, p. 127.

THE TABLE PRAYER

PREFACE:
"Prayer of Thanksgiving," *The Experimental Liturgy Book,*
p. 76.

HYMN OF PRAISE:
"Sing Praise to Our Creator," third verse, *People's Mass Book,*
#43.

ACCLAMATION AT CONSECRATION:
"Keep in Mind," *People's Mass Book,* #145.

ENDING ACCLAMATION:
#190b, *People's Mass Book.*

THE SERVICE OF COMMUNION

THE "OUR FATHER"

RITE OF PEACE

FRACTION RITE:
Litany of the "Lamb of God"

SONG:
"O Taste and See the Goodness of the Lord" (Ps. 33), *Psalms for Singing*, Book I, p. 14.

PERIOD OF REFLECTION:
Intermission

THE DISMISSAL RITE

PRAYER OF BENEDICTION:
Eucharistic Liturgies, p. 127. Omit first and third sentences.

BLESSING AND DISMISSAL

ANNOUNCEMENTS

RECESSIONAL:
"Now Thank We All Our God," *People's Mass Book*, #178.

TWENTIETH SUNDAY AFTER PENTECOST I

Theme: Christian Unity and Marriage

THE ENTRANCE RITE

PROCESSIONAL:
"We Gather Together," *People's Mass Book,* #53.

GREETING:
Eucharistic Liturgies, p. 128.

PRAYER OF INVOCATION:
Eucharistic Liturgies, p. 128. Omit third sentence.

THE SERVICE OF THE WORD

FIRST READING:
Genesis 2:18–24.

RESPONSE:
Rod McKuen in *Listen to Love,* p. 246. Insert "Eternal Father" after "I love you . . ."

SECOND READING:
Hebrews 2:9–11.

GOSPEL ACCLAMATION:
"Your Word, O Lord," *Biblical Hymns and Psalms,* Vol. II, p. 88. This is sung by cantor; people respond with "Alleluia, Alleluia" as indicated.

THE GOSPEL:
Mark 10:2–16.

GOSPEL ACCLAMATION:
"Alleluia, Alleluia," as indicated in Gospel Acclamation above.

HOMILY

GENERAL INTENTIONS:

(*Response:* O Lord, hear our prayer.)

That all married Christians remember that they are living signs of the union of the Church with our Father in heaven, we pray to the Lord:

That all adults, whether married or single, may never be lonely, we pray to the Lord:

That people may be generous and honest toward one another, we pray to the Lord:

That our young people, whose lives lie ahead of them, may learn to live together with all of life's uncertainties, we pray to the Lord:

That all people who belong to each other may go through life together, we pray to the Lord:

PERIOD OF REFLECTION:

Intermission

PROCESSIONAL:

"Bring to the Lord Your Offering" (Ps. 28, Antiphon III), *Twenty-Four Psalms and a Canticle*, p. 14.

PRAYER OF BLESSING OVER GIFTS:

Eucharistic Liturgies, p. 129.

THE TABLE PRAYER

PREFACE:

"Eucharistic Prayer of Human Unity," *The Experimental Liturgy Book*, p. 100.

HYMN OF PRAISE:

"Holy, Holy, Holy! Lord God Almighty," *People's Mass Book*, #184.

ACCLAMATION AT CONSECRATION:

#235a, *People's Mass Book.*

ENDING ACCLAMATION:

#190b, *People's Mass Book.*

THE SERVICE OF COMMUNION

THE "OUR FATHER"

RITE OF PEACE

FRACTION RITE:
    Litany of the "Lamb of God"

SONG:
    "They'll Know We Are Christians by Our Love," *Hymnal for Young Christians*, p. 132.

PERIOD OF REFLECTION:
    Intermission

THE DISMISSAL RITE

PRAYER OF BENEDICTION:
    Eucharistic Liturgies, p. 129.

BLESSING AND DISMISSAL

ANNOUNCEMENTS

RECESSIONAL:
    "All Glory, Praise, and Honor," *People's Mass Book*, #29.

TWENTY-FIRST SUNDAY AFTER PENTECOST I

Theme: Wisdom, God's Gift to the Faithful

THE ENTRANCE RITE

INVITATION TO WORSHIP:
   "Wisdom of Solomon" in *Listen to Love*, p. 281, beginning with
   "The Beginning of wisdom. . . ."

PROCESSIONAL:
   "Priestly People," *People's Mass Book*, #146.

GREETING:
   Eucharistic Liturgies, p. 130.

PRAYER OF INVOCATION:
   Eucharistic Liturgies, p. 130.

THE SERVICE OF THE WORD

FIRST READING:
   Wisdom 7:7–11.

RESPONSE:
   Ps. 90:14–17.

SECOND READING:
   Hebrews 4:12–13.

RESPONSE:
   "Autumn Prayer" in *Listen to Love*, p. 271.

GOSPEL ACCLAMATION:
   "Alleluia, Alleluia, Alleluia," *People's Mass Book*, #86c.

THE GOSPEL:
   Mark 10:17–30.

GOSPEL ACCLAMATION:
   Repeat from above.

HOMILY

GENERAL INTENTIONS:
   (*Response:* O Lord, hear our prayer.)
   That all Christian people of the world try harder to
      seek your wisdom, we pray to the Lord:
   That we may be more tolerant of our brothers' views
      and opinions that differ from our own, we pray to the Lord:
   That the world's leaders, in their wisdom, may at long last
      bring world peace, we pray to the Lord:
   That touched by the joy of wisdom, we may see the light
      of Christ in one another, we pray to the Lord:

PERIOD OF REFLECTION:
   Intermission

PROCESSIONAL:
   "Praise God, From Whom All Blessings Flow," *People's Mass
   Book,* #45.

PRAYER OF BLESSING OVER GIFTS:
   Eucharistic Liturgies, p. 131.

THE TABLE PRAYER

PREFACE:
   "Unity Preface," *The Experimental Liturgy Book,* p. 27.

HYMN OF PRAISE:
   "Holy, Holy, Holy," *People's Mass Book,* #106.

ACCLAMATION AT CONSECRATION:
   #235a, *People's Mass Book.*

ENDING ACCLAMATION:
   #108b, *People's Mass Book.*

THE SERVICE OF COMMUNION

THE "OUR FATHER"

RITE OF PEACE

FRACTION RITE:
Litany of the "Lamb of God"

SONG:
"My Shepherd Is the Lord" (Ps. 22, Antiphon I), *Twenty-Four Psalms and a Canticle*, p. 10.

PERIOD OF REFLECTION:
Intermission

THE DISMISSAL RITE

PRAYER OF BENEDICTION:
Eucharistic Liturgies, p. 129.

BLESSING AND DISMISSAL

ANNOUNCEMENTS

RECESSIONAL:
"A Mighty Fortress Is Our God," *People's Mass Book*, #187.

TWENTY-SECOND SUNDAY AFTER PENTECOST I

Theme: "Serve the Lord With Gladness"

THE ENTRANCE RITE

INVITATION TO WORSHIP:
Vatican Council II in *Faces of Freedom*, p. 125.

PROCESSIONAL:
"All the Earth," *People's Mass Book*, #141.

GREETING:
Eucharistic Liturgies, p. 132.

PRAYER OF INVOCATION:
Father, we live in this world surrounded by values
    that often conflict.
There are forces strong about us
    to weaken our faith in you,
    to move us to hatred and unconcern,
    and to cause us to be afraid.
Yet we are the people of your promise
    whose sole meaning is
    to speak your love to men,
    to show by our lives that you have sent us.
We ask you to be with us, Father,
    as we move through time on our way to you,
    to be our strength and refuge for all times to come.
So may men come to know and believe
    that you are our God, now and forever.
(First sentence from *Eucharistic Liturgies*, p. 132.)

THE SERVICE OF THE WORD

FIRST READING:
Isaiah 45:1, 4–6.

RESPONSE:
Wisdom 1:1–3.

SECOND READING:
2 Timothy 3:14–17.

RESPONSE:
2 Timothy 4:1–2. Omit "I put this duty to you" and insert "we must" before "proclaim" and before "refute."

GOSPEL ACCLAMATION:
"Alleluia! Alleluia," *Biblical Hymns and Psalms,* p. 86.

THE GOSPEL:
Matthew 22:15–21.

GOSPEL ACCLAMATION:
Repeat from above.

HOMILY

GENERAL INTENTIONS:
(*Response:* Lord, hear our prayer.)
Intentions should consist of prayers for current local, national, and world needs.

PERIOD OF REFLECTION:
Intermission

PROCESSIONAL:
"Arise, Come To Your God" (Ps. 99, Antiphon I), *Twenty-Four Psalms and a Canticle,* p. 32.

PRAYER OF BLESSING OVER GIFTS:
Eucharistic Liturgies, p. 133.

THE TABLE PRAYER

PREFACE:
   "Canon of Christian Service," *The Experimental Liturgy Book,*
   p. 66.

HYMN OF PRAISE:
   "Praise God, From Whom All Blessings Flow," *People's Mass
   Book,* #45.

ACCLAMATION AT CONSECRATION:
   #235a, *People's Mass Book.*

ENDING ACCLAMATION:
   "You Alone Are Holy," *Biblical Hymns and Psalms,* Vol. II,
   p. 52.

THE SERVICE OF COMMUNION

THE "OUR FATHER"

RITE OF PEACE

FRACTION RITE:
   Litany of the "Lamb of God"

SONG:
   "Wisdom Has Built Herself a House," *People's Mass Book,*
   #172.

PERIOD OF REFLECTION:
   Intermission

THE DISMISSAL RITE

PRAYER OF BENEDICTION:
   Eucharistic Liturgies, p. 133.

BLESSING AND DISMISSAL

ANNOUNCEMENTS

RECESSIONAL:
   "Sing Praise to Our Creator," *People's Mass Book,* #43.

TWENTY-THIRD SUNDAY AFTER PENTECOST I

Theme: A Celebration of God's Mercy

THE ENTRANCE RITE

INVITATION TO WORSHIP:
> Portia's "Mercy speech" (Act IV, Scene i, lines 184–189,
> 194–197, 200–202) from "The Merchant of Venice," *The Living
> Shakespeare*, p. 298.

PROCESSIONAL:
> "All the Earth," *People's Mass Book*, #141.

GREETING:
> Rejoice in the Lord, for he has been good to us;
> the earth is filled with the kindness of our God.

PRAYER OF INVOCATION:
> *Eucharistic Liturgies*, p. 124.

THE SERVICE OF THE WORD

FIRST READING:
> Jeremiah 31:7–9. Introduction: "We live in an atmosphere of
> mercy . . ." (this one sentence) from *A New Catechism*,
> p. 454, under the topic, "Forgiveness."

RESPONSE:
> Ps. 126:1–2a, 2b–3, 4–5,6 (*by reader*).
> "The Lord has done great things for us, and we are filled
> with joy" (*by people—alternated with verses from Ps. 126,
> cited above*).

SECOND READING:
> Hebrews 5:1–6.

GOSPEL ACCLAMATION:
> "Alleluia! Alleluia!," *Biblical Hymns and Psalms*, p. 86.

THE GOSPEL:
   Mark 10:46–52.

GOSPEL ACCLAMATION:
   Repeat from above.

HOMILY

GENERAL INTENTIONS:
   (*Response:* Father of mercy, hear our prayer.)
   That we may realize that God does not give his mercy
      to us for ourselves alone; that his compassion must overflow
      from us and help other men rejoice in his great mercy, we
      pray to the Lord:
   For kind and compassionate treatment of those who may
      offend us; for the lonely, the aged, the youth afflicted with
      drug abuse, the sick, the dying, we pray to the Lord:
   For families and relatives of defendants in our jails who have
      no resources for furnishing bond or for skilled defense
      attorneys to represent them in court, we pray to the Lord:
   For those soon to be released from prison, that God's mercy
      dominate the quality of our mercy, so that we cast aside
      the label of "ex-convict" and regard them as men, as they
      come to live and work in our community, we pray to the
      Lord:
   In thanksgiving for God's mercy to his people, let us pray
      to the Lord:

PERIOD OF REFLECTION:
   Intermission

PROCESSIONAL:
   "We Give You Thanks," *People's Mass Book*, #190b.

PRAYER OF BLESSING OVER GIFTS:
   Eucharistic Liturgies, p. 86.

THE TABLE PRAYER

PREFACE:
"The Canon of Christian Hope," *The Experimental Liturgy Book*, p. 71.

HYMN OF PRAISE:
"Praise the Lord of Heaven," *People's Mass Book*, #180.

ACCLAMATION AT CONSECRATION:
"Keep in Mind," *People's Mass Book*, #145.

ENDING ACCLAMATION:
#190b, *People's Mass Book*.

THE SERVICE OF COMMUNION

THE "OUR FATHER"

RITE OF PEACE

FRACTION RITE:
Litany of the "Lamb of God"

SONG:
"At the Lamb's High Feast," *Our Parish Prays and Sings*, #2.

PERIOD OF REFLECTION:
Intermission

THE DISMISSAL RITE

PRAYER OF BENEDICTION:
Eucharistic Liturgies, p. 90.

BLESSING AND DISMISSAL

ANNOUNCEMENTS

RECESSIONAL:
"For All the Saints," *The Hymnal of the Protestant Episcopal Church in the United States of America*, #126.

TWENTY-FOURTH SUNDAY AFTER PENTECOST I

Theme: Commitment

THE ENTRANCE RITE

INVITATION TO WORSHIP:
Mathew Fox in *Discovery in Prayer*, pp. 53–54.

PROCESSIONAL:
"We Gather Together," *People's Mass Book*, #53.

GREETING:
Blessings to you of faith,
    who by baptism have chosen to convert yourselves
    from lives of service to self
    to lives of service to our God, dwelling among men,
The Spirit of the Lord be with you.

PRAYER OF INVOCATION:
Aware that as a graced people we are ever deepening our
    commitment to our God and Father, let us pray:
Ever-present Father, we gather in gratitude
    to feed upon your Word, Jesus;
    to be strengthened by him,
    to be drawn out of our walled-up selves
    so that we may enter ever more deeply into the
    life he has offered to share.
To accept that life we must be willing to pay the
    price of self-sacrifice.
Give us courage and faith to say "yes" to this invitation.
We ask this through Jesus Christ your Son
    whose eternal "yes" is ever with us by his Spirit,
    living forever and ever.

THE SERVICE OF THE WORD

FIRST READING:
1 Kings 17:10–16.

RESPONSE:
>   Ps. 146:6a–7, 8a–9b, 8c–10 (*by reader*). "All You On Earth,"
>   *People's Mass Book*, #142 (*antiphon sung by people—alter-
>   nated with verses from Ps. 146, cited above.*)

THE GOSPEL:
>   Mark 13:41–44.

HOMILY

GENERAL INTENTIONS:
>   (*Response:* Lord, hear our prayer.)
>   For those who spend their lives in service to this community,
>   trying to make it a truly human place to live, let us pray
>   to the Lord:
>   For those frightened of decisions, for those who are confused
>   and lonely, let us pray to the Lord:
>   For all who have been alienated, imprisoned, exiled, and
>   hospitalized, that our oneness with them can become known
>   as we seek to be more compassionate, let us pray to the
>   Lord:
>   For all those we know who have become hardened and bitter
>   persons, and for those who work to keep us gentle, let
>   us pray to the Lord:

PERIOD OF REFLECTION:
>   Intermission

PROCESSIONAL:
>   "Grant to Us," *Biblical Hymns and Psalms*, p. 40.

PRAYER OF BLESSING OVER GIFTS:
>   Loving Father, you have, by your Son,
>   opened yourself to mankind.
>   By these gifts we seek to open ourselves too,
>   so that we can risk ourselves to grow
>   ever deeper in the mystery of love.
>   We tremble at the thought of the cost,

but take us, nonetheless, and make us into your
faithful image.
We ask this through Jesus Christ, your Son, and the Spirit,
who live with you forever and ever.

THE TABLE PRAYER

PREFACE:
"The Canon of the Pilgrim Church," *The Experimental Liturgy
Book,* p. 73.

HYMN OF PRAISE:
"Praise to the Lord," third verse, *People's Mass Book,* #175.

ACCLAMATION AT CONSECRATION:
#190b, *People's Mass Book.*

ENDING ACCLAMATION:
#108b, *People's Mass Book.*

THE SERVICE OF COMMUNION

THE "OUR FATHER"

RITE OF PEACE

FRACTION RITE:
Litany of the "Lamb of God"

SONG:
"Alleluia! Sing to Jesus," *The Hymnal of the Protestant
Episcopal Church in the United States of America,* #347.

PERIOD OF REFLECTION:
Intermission

THE DISMISSAL RITE

PRAYER OF BENEDICTION:

(Recited with congregation.) Dennis Coraddo in *Discovery in Prayer*, pp. 54–55.

BLESSING AND DISMISSAL

ANNOUNCEMENTS

RECESSIONAL:

"Rejoice, The Lord Is King," *Hymnal for Young Christians*, p. 115.

TWENTY-FIFTH SUNDAY AFTER PENTECOST I

Theme: Enlightenment

THE ENTRANCE RITE

INVITATION TO WORSHIP:
First two paragraphs, p. 49, John H. McGoey, *The Sins of the Just*. Change feminine pronouns to masculine.

PROCESSIONAL:
"Send Forth Your Light and Your Truth" (Ps. 42, Antiphon II), *Twenty-Four Psalms and a Canticle*, p. 20.

GREETING:
May the God of all light and truth
   who has shared the knowledge of himself with us
   through the revelation of his Son, Jesus,
   be with us and give us his peace.

PRAYER OF INVOCATION:
As a people striving to come out of the darkness toward
   the light offered to us by the Lord, let us pray:
Heavenly Father, we know that you are light and wisdom itself
   before any other light was.
You sent your Son as light into the world,
   but we preferred darkness to light because our deeds
   were evil.
Grant, Father, that we may change our attitudes
   and ever seek you as the light
   and so be in your presence forever and ever.
(First sentence of prayer adapted from "Liturgy of the Lord
of Light," *The Experimental Liturgy Book*, p. 109.)

THE SERVICE OF THE WORD

FIRST READING:
Karl Rahner in *Discovery in Prayer*, pp. 25–26, first paragraph
only.

RESPONSE:
Ps. 128: 1–2, 4–5b (*by reader*).
"Happy are those who fear the Lord" (*by people—alternating with verses of Ps. 128, cited above*).

SECOND READING:
1 Thessalonians 5:1–6.

GOSPEL ACCLAMATION:
"Alleluia! Alleluia!," *Biblical Hymns and Psalms,* p. 86.

THE GOSPEL:
Matthew 25:14–30.

GOSPEL ACCLAMATION:
Repeat from above.

HOMILY

GENERAL INTENTIONS:
(*Response:* O Lord, hear our prayer.)
That all who have forsaken the life offered to us by God,
    our Father, may have the courage to acknowledge their
    isolation from God and seek to return to his love by means
    of the sacrament of penance, let us pray to the Lord:
That all who are sharing the life of God may experience a
    continuing process of conversion to the Lord each time they
    encounter Jesus in the sacrament of penance, let us pray
    to the Lord:
That we might come to understand that our own seeking for
    forgiveness will end in the very process of our forgiving
    others, let us pray to the Lord:

PERIOD OF REFLECTION:
Intermission

PROCESSIONAL:
"Arise, Come to Your God" (Ps. 99, Antiphon I), *Twenty-Four
Psalms and a Canticle,* p. 32.

PRAYER OF BLESSING OVER GIFTS:
>God our Father, we, your people, come to this altar-table
>>to offer you bread and wine
>>as a sign of our thankfulness
>>for all that we have and all that we are.
>As we reflect on our uniqueness and the individual talents
>>we each have to enrich our lives and the lives of others,
>>we pledge ourselves to you by these gifts.
>Be pleased with us and, in return,
>>fill us with your life and joy.
>We ask this, Father, in your Son's name,
>>he who with you and the Spirit,
>>lives as God, forever and ever.

THE TABLE PRAYER

PREFACE:
>"Liturgy of the Lord of Light," *The Experimental Liturgy Book*, p. 109.

HYMN OF PRAISE:
>"Holy, Holy, Holy! Lord God Almighty," third verse, *People's Mass Book*, #184.

ACCLAMATION AT CONSECRATION:
>"Keep in Mind," *People's Mass Book*, #145.

ENDING ACCLAMATION:
>#190b, *People's Mass Book*.

THE SERVICE OF COMMUNION

THE "OUR FATHER"

RITE OF PEACE

FRACTION RITE:
>Litany of the "Lamb of God"

SONG:
"Grant to Us," *Biblical Hymns and Psalms*, p. 40.

PERIOD OF REFLECTION:
Intermission

THE DISMISSAL RITE

PRAYER OF BENEDICTION:
Father, we thank you for your Word which has given us light.
We thank you for other men
who constantly enlighten us
by their words and their lives.
May we, also, by the strength of the Bread of the Eucharist,
become a light unto others
so that they may see you in the world
and so come to believe.
We ask this, Father, in the strength of your Son's name,
he who, with you and the Spirit, lives as God,
forever and ever.

BLESSING AND DISMISSAL

ANNOUNCEMENTS

RECESSIONAL:
"Now Thank We All Our God," *People's Mass Book*, #178.

FESTIVAL OF THE ASSUMPTION I

Theme: A Living Sign of Hope

THE ENTRANCE RITE

INVITATION TO WORSHIP:
Section VIII, Paragraph 59, *The Constitution of the Church of Vatican Council II.*

GREETING:
Eucharistic Liturgies, p. 117.

PRAYER OF INVOCATION:
Mindful of our call to be real believers and
    remembering Mary as the greatest of believers, let us pray:
O God, your name has been with us
    from the beginning,
    a Word full of promise to keep us going.
We celebrate your goodness and might,
    for you have given us Mary,
    the pride of Israel, the flower of our race.
She is the sign of all we need to be and can be—
    persons full of faith,
    persons who recognize your presence
    and make this presence felt in our world.
We praise you now, together with your Son, Jesus,
    and the Spirit, forever and ever.

THE SERVICE OF THE WORD

FIRST READING:
Judith 13:18(23)–20(25); 14: 9b(10b)–10(11). Begin with
"May you be blessed . . ." and omit "by whose guidance
you cut off the head of the leader of our enemy." Begin
second excerpt with "You are the glory. . . ."

RESPONSE:
Colossians 1:9a–12. Start with "We ask God . . . that through

perfect wisdom. . . ." Change "you" and "your" to "we,"
"us," or "our" throughout passage.

SECOND READING:
    Omitted today.

GOSPEL ACCLAMATION:
    "Alleluia! Alleluia," *Biblical Hymns and Psalms*, p. 86.

THE GOSPEL:
    Mark 3:31–35.

GOSPEL ACCLAMATION:
    Repeat from above.

HOMILY

GENERAL INTENTIONS:
    (*Response:* Lord, hear our prayer.)
    Selection from p. 142 and first paragraph, p. 143, *Your Word
    Is Near.*

PERIOD OF REFLECTION:
    Intermission

PROCESSIONAL:
    "Of My Hands," *Hymnal for Young Christians*, p. 79.

PRAYER OF BLESSING OVER GIFTS:
    Father, we set our prayers and our needs before you,
        and offer you all that we are.
    We will break bread together, for one another,
        as Christ, your Son, has invited us to do.
    Strengthen us now that we may live together
        in peace, in harmony and love.
    Make us one with Jesus Christ
        that he may be present wherever we speak,
        that his hand may bless whatever we touch.
    So may we give you praise and thanks
        today and every day, now and forever.

THE TABLE PRAYER

PREFACE:
> Begin with first 12 lines of "The San Miguelito Liturgy,"
> *The Experimental Liturgy Book*, p. 73. Add the following:
> When we had abandoned you adulterously
> > and killed your prophets,
> > we became once more a desert of dry bones.
> But you breathed your Spirit and transformed
> > the womb of the young girl, Mary,
> > into the living temple for your own Son.
> We praise you for the wonders performed in Mary,
> > for she has become the sign of our learning to say,
> > "Let it be," to the wonders performed in us.
> Anxious for a full springtime
> > in all of our nature and in ourselves,
> > we come to you singing:

HYMN OF PRAISE:
> "Praise to the Lord," *People's Mass Book*, #175.

ACCLAMATION AT CONSECRATION:
> #235a, *People's Mass Book*.

ENDING ACCLAMATION:
> "You Alone Are Holy," *Biblical Hymns and Psalms*, Vol. II,
> p. 52.

THE SERVICE OF COMMUNION

THE "OUR FATHER"

RITE OF PEACE

FRACTION RITE:
> Litany of the "Lamb of God"

SONG:
> Omitted today. After meditation period, all recite together
> "Mary's Song of Thanksgiving," *Your Word Is Near*, p. 53.

PERIOD OF REFLECTION:
   Intermission

THE DISMISSAL RITE

PRAYER OF BENEDICTION:
   "We have your promise, God," *Your Word Is Near*, p. 62.

BLESSING AND DISMISSAL

ANNOUNCEMENTS

RECESSIONAL:
   "Keep in Mind," *People's Mass Book*, #145.

FESTIVAL OF ALL SAINTS I

Theme: A Variety of Gifts in One Spirit

THE ENTRANCE RITE

INVITATION TO WORSHIP:
Reader: On this festival of all the saints, we come to worship
the Lord. He is our God, and we are his people. This we
remember and now pray together: Worthy is the Lamb that
has been slain to receive power and riches, might, honor, glory
and blessing.
People: Unto the Lamb of God be all glory!
Reader: Worthy are you, for you purchased unto God with your
blood, men of every tribe and tongue and people and nation.
People: Unto the Lamb of God be all glory! Honor and power be
his, forever and ever.
Reader: Worthy is the Lamb who has had shining witnesses
through the ages; let us praise him and his deeds of glory
with exultation.
People: It is right and just for us to rejoice in the Lamb of
God and all his saints.
(Adapted from Revelation 4:9–14.)

PROCESSIONAL:
"For All the Saints," *The Hymnal of the Protestant Episcopal
Church in the United States of America,* #126.

GREETING:
Strength and blessings be yours from God our Father,
whose spirit moves in our midst
to open our eyes and unlock our hearts
so that we follow his Son to the glory of all the saints.
May the Spirit of the Lord be with you.

PRAYER OF INVOCATION:
Mindful that we too are called to be numbered among
the saints, we pray:

Father, today we celebrate the glory of your Son Jesus,
  his victory over sin and weakness;
  we hail with festivity
  all those people of our own flesh and blood
  who have made this victory of Christ their own,
  and who now share his glory.
Father, you have chosen us to be holy and blameless,
  destined to be your sons so that in love
  we serve you and your world as did Jesus.
For this we praise you through him who lives with the Spirit,
  forever and ever.

THE SERVICE OF THE WORD

FIRST READING:
Revelation 7:9–17.

RESPONSE:
We thank you, God, with all our heart that the Spirit of life
has set us and our ancestors free from the law of sin and
death. For you have done what mere advice or commands
could not do. In sending your Son in the likeness of sinful
flesh, you have given us strength and power to walk not
according to discord, selfishness and self-pity, but along the
way of faith, joy, mutual support and compassion. If we live
in your friendship, then we live with assurance that a new
life awaits us which is beyond imagination.
(Adapted from "Liberty and Life," *Prayers from St. Paul.*)

SECOND READING:
Entry for January 16, 1923, *Journal of a Soul,* p. 106.

GOSPEL ACCLAMATION:
"Alleluia, Alleluia, Alleluia," *People's Mass Book,* #86c. Sing
before and after reading the following:
Father, there are varieties of gifts, but the same Spirit.
And there are varieties of service, but it is always you whom
we serve. And there are varieties of working, but it is the
same God who inspires them all. Through your Spirit, to one

words of wisdom are granted; to another, knowledge; to
another, faith; to another, gifts of healing; to another, working
of signs. You have given us life and we believe that by
living as you call us, doing the work to which we are called,
we will live forever with you. We are heirs with Christ, and
provided we suffer with him, we will be glorified with him.
(Adapted from 1 Corinthians 4–11.)

THE GOSPEL:
  Matthew 5:1–12.

GOSPEL ACCLAMATION:
  Repeat "Alleluia, Alleluia, Alleluia," from above.

HOMILY

GENERAL INTENTIONS:
  (*Response:* All glory and praise to you, our God and Father,
  forever and ever.)
  Selection from pp. 112–113, *Your Word Is Near.*

PERIOD OF REFLECTION:
  Intermission

PROCESSIONAL:
  "Priestly People," *People's Mass Book,* #146.

PRAYER OF BLESSING OVER GIFTS:
  "We thank you for the language of men," *Your Word Is Near,*
  p. 112.

THE TABLE PRAYER

PREFACE:
  It is right to give him thanks and praise.
  We thank you, good Father, for giving us this day
    to remember your greatness in all your people,
    to live for you, together with each other.
  You have invited us to be good people,
    to accomplish our task in life.

You have sent Jesus into this world
    to mold the divine gifts of your people
    into the members of your one family.
He comes constantly in our midst
    to go before us and show us the way to you.
You have such patience with us,
    even when we stumble and fall along the way.
The whole earth you have entrusted to us,
    to make it a dwelling filled with joy and peace,
    a place where people might grow
    and reflect the fulfillment of your kingdom.
Confident that you accept us in our innermost selves,
    with all the living we sing your praise:

HYMN OF PRAISE:
    "Holy God, We Praise Thy Name," *People's Mass Book*, #176.

ACCLAMATION AT CONSECRATION:
    #235a, *People's Mass Book*.

ENDING ACCLAMATION:
    "You Alone Are Holy," *Biblical Hymns and Psalms*, Vol. II,
    p. 52.

THE SERVICE OF COMMUNION

THE "OUR FATHER"

RITE OF PEACE

FRACTION RITE:
    Litany of the "Lamb of God"

SONG:
    "All Men On Earth," *People's Mass Book*, #36.

PERIOD OF REFLECTION:
    Intermission

THE DISMISSAL RITE

PRAYER OF BENEDICTION:
>   Lord, through your Spirit alive in us,
>   give a new face to our old world.
>   Count us among your saints
>   and make of us a splendid array of witnesses
>   so that we serve you and your world
>   with complete dependence on you,
>   and with a taste of the victory of Jesus Christ.
>   We ask this through Jesus victorious,
>   and his Spirit living among us forever and ever.

BLESSING AND DISMISSAL

ANNOUNCEMENTS

RECESSIONAL:
>   "A Mighty Fortress Is Our God," *People's Mass Book,* #187.

THE FESTIVAL OF CHRIST, KING

Theme: "He Is Among Us Whom We Do Not Know"

THE ENTRANCE RITE

INVITATION TO WORSHIP:
  "The song of the Lord in our midst," *Your Word Is Near,*
  p. 144; the people join in reading the last line of each stanza.

PROCESSIONAL:
  "To Jesus Christ, Our Sovereign King," *People's Mass Book,*
  #48.

GREETING:
  Blessings to you, faithful people, as we gather to praise
  the Father who has called us to bear his name to all
  mankind as leaders in the fellowship of his Son, Christ
  our King.

PRAYER OF INVOCATION:
  "You are the voice of the living God," *Your Word Is Near,*
  p. 97.

THE SERVICE OF THE WORD

FIRST READING:
  Martin Luther King in *Faces of Freedom,* p. 90.

RESPONSE:
  Silent reflection.

SECOND READING:
  Daniel 7:13–14.

RESPONSE:
  "Praise be to Jesus Christ, the faithful witness . . ."; continue
  with Revelation 1:5–6.

212

GOSPEL ACCLAMATION:
#86c, *People's Mass Book.*

THE GOSPEL:
Luke 19:35–38. Continue with, "Later it happened that Pilate
put to him this question." Continue with John 18:37.

GOSPEL ACCLAMATION:
Repeat from above.

HOMILY

GENERAL INTENTIONS:
(*Response:* Lord, hear our prayer.)
For all our fellow men, that together we may find
    the humility to lead ourselves and each other to the
    true kingdom of God, we pray to the Lord:
For ourselves that, young or old, we may constantly be made
    new men by the Father's grace, we pray to the Lord:
For compassion and affection from those around us; that
    being ever made new and gentle, we might offer the same
    in return, let us pray to the Lord:
For the faithful departed, that they now enjoy the happiness
    of the kingdom of God, we pray to the Lord:

PERIOD OF REFLECTION:
Intermission

PROCESSIONAL:
"Priestly People," *People's Mass Book,* #146.

PRAYER OF BLESSING OVER GIFTS:
Lord Jesus, we your people have accepted you
    as our King, as our leader in life.
You have led us in such a manner
    that unless we are continually conscious of you
    in our brother
    we will never really be with you.
By this offering of bread and wine,

we pledge our loyalty and service to you, our King,
  as we serve the needs of those about us.
Together with you we offer thanks to God our Father,
  who with the Spirit, lives and rules forever and ever.

THE TABLE PRAYER

PREFACE:
Preface for Christ the King in *The English-Latin Sacramentary.*

HYMN OF PRAISE:
"Praise God, From Whom All Blessings Flow," *People's Mass Book*, #45.

ACCLAMATION AT CONSECRATION:
"Keep in Mind," *People's Mass Book*, #145.

ENDING ACCLAMATION:
"You Alone Are Holy," *Biblical Hymns and Psalms*, Vol. II, p. 52.

THE SERVICE OF COMMUNION

THE "OUR FATHER"

RITE OF PEACE

FRACTION RITE:
Litany of the "Lamb of God"

SONG:
"All Glory, Praise, and Honor," *People's Mass Book*, #29.

PERIOD OF REFLECTION:
Intermission

THE DISMISSAL RITE

PRAYER OF BENEDICTION:

> God our Father, we give you thanks
>> for the words we have heard,
>> the Bread we have shared.
> Grant that as we go forth into our world
>> the power of these things may work in us.
> Let us truly live as the servants of Christ, our King,
>> so that we may extend the power and wisdom
>> of his presence to all whom we meet.
> We ask this, Father, as we pray in your Son's name,
>> he who with you and the Spirit, is living as God,
>> forever and ever.

BLESSING AND DISMISSAL

ANNOUNCEMENTS

RECESSIONAL:

> "Sion, Sing," *People's Mass Book,* #165.

FESTIVAL OF THANKSGIVING I

Theme: Thanks and Giving

THE ENTRANCE RITE

INVITATION TO WORSHIP:
Excerpt from "History of the Pilgrim Colony," *The
Experimental Liturgy Book*, p. 174.

PROCESSIONAL:
"Faith of Our Fathers," *People's Mass Book*, #188.

GREETING:
Eucharistic Liturgies, p. 141.

PRAYER OF INVOCATION:
With grateful hearts for all that we are in this life, let us pray:
Almighty God, we thank you for your loving kindness
    to us and to all mankind.
In your action of creation
    you have shared with man your very life and power.
Above all, you have shown your love for man
    be revealing yourself and your will through
    your Son, Jesus.
May we praise and thank you always,
    not only with our lips but in our very lives,
    by serving our fellow man in kindness and justice
    all the days of our lives.
This we ask in the name of Jesus,
    who with you and the Holy Spirit,
    is living as God, forever and ever.

THE SERVICE OF THE WORD

FIRST READING:
Romans 12:6–8.

RESPONSE:
Ps. 98:1–8.

SECOND READING:
Omitted today.

GOSPEL ACCLAMATION:
"Alleluia! Alleluia," *Biblical Hymns and Psalms*, p. 86.

THE GOSPEL:
John 15:1–8.

GOSPEL ACCLAMATION:
Repeat from above.

HOMILY

GENERAL INTENTIONS:
(*Response:* O Lord, let us show that our thankfulness is
sincere by using our gifts for the joy of others.)
As we are thankful for all that we have received in this
    life, let us be mindful of others who are less fortunate
    than we are. Let our prayers of thanksgiving be meaningful
    as we use our gifts to improve the quality of life of all
    those about us; let us pray to the Lord:
As we are thankful for the joy of friends and family on this
    day, may our happiness be shared with others by a smile,
    a cheerful word of greeting, a small act of courtesy, a visit;
    let us pray to the Lord:
As we are thankful for our freedom and the respect of our
    human dignity, may we be unfailing in our efforts to see
    that all men of this city and of this nation have the same
    reasons to be thankful; let us pray to the Lord:
As we are thankful for our abilities to learn, may we ever
    strive to grow in our knowledge of Jesus' word so that it
    may transform us into living witnesses of his love and
    concern for all men; let us pray to the Lord:
As we are thankful for the food on our tables let us constantly

use the strength of that food in service to others; let us pray
to the Lord:

PERIOD OF REFLECTION:
Intermission

PROCESSIONAL:
"We Gather Together," *People's Mass Book,* #53.

PRAYER OF BLESSING OVER GIFTS:
Eucharistic Liturgies, p. 141. Omit second sentence.

THE TABLE PRAYER

PREFACE:
"Canon for a Day of Thanksgiving," *Eucharistic Liturgies,*
p. 199. After "have made it great" (third sentence), add,
"We thank you for men of genius who work wonders in our
behalf, for the unnoticed men and women who contribute
daily to our welfare." After "each breath we draw" add "We
thank you for children's smiles and the vision of youth, for the
love in parents' eyes." After "give you thanks" add ". . . by
our wise and constant use of your gifts to us."

HYMN OF PRAISE:
"Praise God, From Whom All Blessings Flow," *People's Mass
Book,* #45.

ACCLAMATION AT CONSECRATION:
#190b, *People's Mass Book.*

ENDING ACCLAMATION:
#108b, *People's Mass Book.*

THE SERVICE OF COMMUNION

THE "OUR FATHER"

RITE OF PEACE

FRACTION RITE:
Litany of the "Lamb of God"

SONG:
"Come and Eat of My Bread" (Antiphon II), *People's Mass Book*, #172.

PERIOD OF REFLECTION:
Intermission

THE DISMISSAL RITE

PRAYER OF BENEDICTION:
Eucharistic Liturgies, p. 142. Omit third and fourth sentences.

BLESSING AND DISMISSAL

ANNOUNCEMENTS

RECESSIONAL:
"Now Thank We All Our God," *People's Mass Book*, #178.

LITURGIES FOR SPECIAL OCCASIONS

Graduation

Marriage

Anniversary of Marriage

Thanksgiving Day

A GRADUATION OR BACCALAUREATE CELEBRATION

THE ENTRANCE RITE

INVITATION TO WORSHIP:

On the night before the Hebrews enslaved in Egypt made their daring break for freedom they gathered together to eat and remember their Lord God. The evening before Jesus Christ began his journey to freedom from death on behalf of us all, he gathered about a table with his loved ones. And so it is in this sacred tradition that the graduating class gathers with its most loved ones to remember all the great things of our past which have brought us to this day in a spirit of gratitude; and we break bread and share the body and the blood of Jesus Christ, the Lord, as a sign of our unity. For it is because of him and our common faith in him that we were first brought together as a Christian people; and it is by this sign that we will, in days and years to come, remember one another even though continents may divide us.

PROCESSIONAL:

"We Gather Together," *People's Mass Book,* #53.

GREETING:

Blessings and peace to you who are here with joy
to celebrate this festival of achievement.
May the Spirit of Christ Jesus who calls us to be one
be with you all.

PRAYER OF INVOCATION:

Two line introduction, *Eucharistic Liturgies,* p. 186; followed by "We are your Church, a people on the way," *Your Word Is Near,* p. 145.

THE SERVICE OF THE WORD

FIRST READING:

"Humanity in Progress," Paragraph 20, *Hymn of the Universe,*
p. 92.

RESPONSE:
Three line introduction on p. 40, followed by quote from
Vatican II, p. 48, in *Horizons of Hope.*

SECOND READING:
Revelation 21:1–4.

GOSPEL ACCLAMATION:
"Alleluia! The Strife Is O'er," second verse, *People's Mass
Book,* #34.

THE GOSPEL:
John 17:13–21.

GOSPEL ACCLAMATION:
"Alleluia! The Strife Is O'er," third verse, *People's Mass Book,*
#34.

HOMILY

GENERAL INTENTIONS:
(*Response:* Lord, hear our prayer.)
Selection from pp. 112–113 and/or 126–127, *Your Word Is
Near.*

PERIOD OF REFLECTION:
Intermission

PROCESSIONAL:
"Priestly People," *People's Mass Book,* #146.

PRAYER OF BLESSING OVER GIFTS:
Only the "Let us pray that my sacrifice and yours . . ."
and its response is used today.

THE TABLE PRAYER

PREFACE:
"Table Prayer 2," *Open Your Hearts,* p. 11.

HYMN OF PRAISE:
"Praise to the Lord," first verse, *People's Mass Book,* #175.

ACCLAMATION AT CONSECRATION:
#235a, *People's Mass Book.*

ENDING ACCLAMATION:
"Praise to the Lord," cited above, third verse.

THE SERVICE OF COMMUNION

THE "OUR FATHER"

RITE OF PEACE

FRACTION RITE:
Litany of the "Lamb of God"

SONG:
Choice of graduating class.

PERIOD OF REFLECTION:
Intermission

THE DISMISSAL RITE

PRAYER OF BENEDICTION:
Eucharistic Liturgies, p. 187.

BLESSING AND DISMISSAL

ANNOUNCEMENTS

RECESSIONAL:
Choice of graduating class.

A CELEBRATION OF
THE SACRAMENT OF MARRIAGE

THE ENTRANCE RITE

PROCESSIONAL:
"Sion Sing," *People's Mass Book*, #165.

GREETING:
The grace and peace of God our Father
and the Lord Jesus Christ be with you.

PRAYER OF INVOCATION:
"The Rite for Celebrating Marriage during Mass," *Manual of Celebration*, p. 4.

THE SERVICE OF THE WORD

FIRST READING:
The Song of Songs 2:8–10, 14, 16a; 8:6–7.
Introduce the last two verses with "He said to me. . . ."

RESPONSE:
A solo: Choice of bride and groom.

SECOND READING:
1 Corinthians 12:31; 13:1–8a.

RESPONSE:
Robert Penn Warren in *Horizons of Hope*, p. 62.

THE GOSPEL:
Mark 10:6–9.

HOMILY

MARRIAGE VOWS, BLESSING AND EXCHANGE OF RINGS:
As in the new *Rite of Marriage*.

GENERAL INTENTIONS:
From page 144, "A Wedding Liturgy," *The Experimental Liturgy Book.*

PERIOD OF REFLECTION:
Intermission

PRAYER OF BLESSING OVER GIFTS:
"The Rite for Celebrating Marriage during Mass," *Manual of Celebration*, p. 13.

THE TABLE PRAYER

PREFACE:
Preface (3), "The Rite for Celebrating Marriage during Mass," *Manual of Celebration*, p. 15.

HYMN OF PRAISE:
"Praise to the Lord," first verse, *People's Mass Book*, #175.

ACCLAMATION AT CONSECRATION:
#235a, *People's Mass Book.*

ENDING ACCLAMATION:
"Praise to the Lord," cited above, third verse.

THE SERVICE OF COMMUNION

THE "OUR FATHER"

THE NUPTIAL BLESSING:
As in the new *Rite of Marriage.*

FRACTION RITE:
Litany of the "Lamb of God"

SONG:
"God Is Love," *Hymnal for Young Christians*, p. 95.

PERIOD OF REFLECTION:
   Intermission

THE DISMISSAL RITE

CREED, WEDDING CREED AND VOWS (a second affirmation):
   Pages 143–144, "A Wedding Liturgy," *The Experimental Liturgy Book.*

BLESSING AND DISMISSAL

RECESSIONAL:
   Organ only.

A CELEBRATION OF THANKSGIVING
ON THE ANNIVERSARY OF MARRIAGE

THE ENTRANCE RITE

INVITATION TO WORSHIP:
Dag Hammarskjold in *The Underground Mass Book*, p. 57.

PROCESSIONAL:
"Priestly People," *People's Mass Book*, #146.

GREETING:
Eucharistic Liturgies, p. 141.

PRAYER OF INVOCATION:
Eucharistic Liturgies, p. 141. Omit "during our past lives and . . ." in the first sentence.

THE SERVICE OF THE WORD

FIRST READING:
Robert Penn Warren in *Horizons of Hope*, p. 64.

RESPONSE:
Silent reflection.

SECOND READING:
Ecclesiasticus 26:1–4, 13(16)–16(21).

RESPONSE:
"Dawning," *Faces of Freedom*, pp. 168–169.

GOSPEL ACCLAMATION:
"Alleluia, Alleluia, Alleluia" (Ps. 150), *People's Mass Book*, #163.

THE GOSPEL:
Matthew 5:1–12a.

227

GOSPEL ACCLAMATION:
"Alleluia, Alleluia, Alleluia," cited above, with an additional verse from Ps. 150.

HOMILY

THE CREED, WEDDING CREED AND VOWS:
"A Wedding Liturgy," *The Experimental Liturgy Book*, p. 143.
All couples present may be asked to join in. The celebrant responds with the following:
May Almighty God bless and sanctify these bonds of marriage, in the name of the Father, and of the Son, and of the Holy Spirit. Amen.

PERIOD OF REFLECTION:
Intermission

PROCESSIONAL:
"We Gather Together," *People's Mass Book*, #53.

PRAYER OF BLESSING OVER GIFTS:
Eucharistic Liturgies, p. 141. Omit second sentence.

THE TABLE PRAYER

PREFACE:
"Canon of the Holy Spirit," *Eucharistic Liturgies*, p. 203.

HYMN OF PRAISE:
"Praise to the Lord," *People's Mass Book*, #175.

ACCLAMATION AT CONSECRATION:
#235a, *People's Mass Book*.

ENDING ACCLAMATION:
"Glory to God, Glory," refrain from "Bless the Lord," *Hymnal for Young Christians*, p. 71.

THE SERVICE OF COMMUNION

THE "OUR FATHER"

RITE OF PEACE

FRACTION RITE:
Litany of the "Lamb of God"

SONG:
"Peace My Friends," *Hymnal for Young Christians*, Vol. II,
p. 34.

PERIOD OF REFLECTION:
Intermission

THE DISMISSAL RITE

PRAYER OF BENEDICTION:
Eucharistic Liturgies, p. 187.

BLESSING AND DISMISSAL:
Philippians 1:9–11.

ANNOUNCEMENTS

RECESSIONAL:
"Sion, Sing," *People's Mass Book*, #165.

FESTIVAL OF THANKSGIVING

Theme: "Lift Up Your Hearts"

THE ENTRANCE RITE

INVITATION TO WORSHIP:
Deuteronomy 26:1–11.

PROCESSIONAL:
"Priestly People," *People's Mass Book*, #146.

GREETING:
The grace of our Lord Jesus Christ
   and the love of God
   and the fellowship of the Holy Spirit
   be with you all.

PRAYER OF INVOCATION:
Entrance Prayer in "A Thanksgiving Liturgy," *The Experimental Liturgy Book*, p. 169.

THE SERVICE OF THE WORD

FIRST READING:
"On Giving," *The Prophet*, pp. 20–21. Use first three sentences; then, "There are those who give little . . ." through next two sentences. Conclude with sentence beginning, "It is well to give when asked. . . ."

RESPONSE:
Ps. 67:1–2, 4, 6–7 (*by reader*). Ps. 67:6 (*by people—alternating with verses given above*).

SECOND READING:
Deuteronomy 8:7–18.

RESPONSE:

230

"Rejoice, The Lord Is King," first verse, *Hymnal for Young Christians*, p. 115.

THE GOSPEL:
Luke 12:15–21.

GOSPEL ACCLAMATION:
"Rejoice, The Lord Is King," cited above, second verse.

PERIOD OF REFLECTION:
Intermission

PROCESSIONAL:
A choral version of the "Magnificat" by the choir; or all may recite together (Luke 1:46–55).

PRAYER OF BLESSING OVER GIFTS:
From "A Thanksgiving Liturgy," *The Experimental Liturgy Book*, p. 171.

THE TABLE PRAYER

PREFACE:
From "A Thanksgiving Liturgy," *The Experimental Liturgy Book*, p. 171.

HYMN OF PRAISE:
"Holy, Holy, Holy! Lord God Almighty," *People's Mass Book*, #184.

ENDING ACCLAMATION:
#190b, *People's Mass Book*.

THE SERVICE OF COMMUNION

THE "OUR FATHER"

RITE OF PEACE

FRACTION RITE:
   Litany of the "Lamb of God"

SONG:
   "All the Earth" (Ps. 100), *People's Mass Book,* #141.

PERIOD OF REFLECTION:
   Intermission

THE DISMISSAL RITE

PRAYER OF BENEDICTION:
   From "A Thanksgiving Liturgy," *The Experimental Liturgy Book,* p. 173.

BLESSING AND DISMISSAL

ANNOUNCEMENTS

RECESSIONAL:
   "Now Thank We All Our God," *People's Mass Book,* #178.

EIGHT LITURGIES
FOR FAMILY CELEBRATION

Theme: Communication

Mother's Day

. Father's Day

Marriage

Anniversary of Marriage

Feast of the Body of Christ

Independence Day

Labor Day

233

Sunday liturgy is a family event-celebration—individual families and the collective parish family. Our special liturgies center around the family in relationship to secular feast days—like Thanksgiving, Labor Day, Mother's Day, Memorial Day. We find these to be more relevant to their lives than the traditional holy-days of obligation. The liturgies take a positive direction and almost always involve relationships, such as mother to dad, mother to children, children to mother, mother to the community.

Home Masses in various areas of the parish are a natural for involving families in informal, personal liturgies, especially at such times as birthdays, anniversaries, homecomings, Baptisms. Masses celebrated twice a week in parish homes—with shared homilies and family themes—deepen liturgical sensibility and help families to more sensitively celebrate the larger formal celebrations on Sundays.

Rev. Bill Skeehan

The next eight liturgies were prepared by Father Skeehan, pastor, and Mary Minden, director of religious education, Church of the Resurrection, Tulsa, Oklahoma.

THEME:
COMMUNICATION WITHIN THE FAMILY

GREETING AND PENITENTIAL RITE

FIRST READING:

How do we live this mystery, how do we unite a family in love? One of the most important things here is the need of communication. First of all, husband and wife should be able to communicate with each other openly and frankly. They must be able to have enough trust in their partner to be able to say what they feel and know that they will be accepted or understood. There is nothing more frightening than for a husband or wife to say that they are afraid to talk something over with their spouse. The doors of communication must always be open if the mystery of life is to be discovered. When the doors close, life closes, and the relationship dries up.

If there is good communication between the parents, then there will also be good communication between the parents and children. Parents who understand each other will be able to understand their children. Children should be able to approach their parents at any time and speak of anything that they want to. If a child is afraid to speak to his parents, then his parents become mere functionaries in his life, and they cease to be parents for him. In order for there to be communication there must be honesty, sincerity, openness, trust; we must not reject or condemn what another says, but only listen and hear what they say.

(From a sermon by Rev. Vincent Krische)

RESPONSE:

"One of a Family," *A New Catechism*, p. 381, first paragraph.

SECOND READING:

James 1:22–25.

SUGGESTED SONGS:

Processional: "They'll Know We Are Christians By Our Love," *Hymnal for Young Christians*, p. 132.

Procession of Gifts: "Yes to You, My Lord," *Hand in Hand*, #12.

Communion: "Priestly People," *People's Mass Book*, #146.

Recessional: "Sent Forth by God's Blessings," *People's Mass Book*, #138.

A CELEBRATION OF MOTHER'S DAY

OPENING:

All assemble in the church or in room suitable for showing slides. During opening song, "Like Olive Branches," slides are shown of family life with special emphasis on the mother.

READINGS:

The congregation separates into different areas according to age level, to listen to their respective readings:

Five-Year-Olds, Kindergarten, and Grade 1: Use an appropriate story showing relation between mother and children.

Grades 2 through 6: Matthew 20:24–28. Chapter 10, *The Little Prince.*

Junior and Senior High: Romans 13:1–6. "Why Teenagers Have Problems," *Discovery in Word,* p. 41.

Adults: Proverbs 31:10–31. "On Children," *The Prophet,* pp. 18–19.

(All reassemble for the celebration of the Eucharist.)

SUGGESTED SONGS:

Processional: "Like Olive Branches," *People's Mass Book,* #159.

Procession of Gifts: "Take Our Bread," *People's Mass Book,* #99.

Communion: "Sons of God," *Hymnal for Young Christians,* p. 98.

Recessional: "All You Peoples, Clap Your Hands," *Hymnal for Young Christians,* p. 62.

A CELEBRATION OF FATHER'S DAY

GREETING AND PENITENTIAL RITE

PRAYER:
> (*All fathers of families are asked to join in*) From pp. 30–31
> of *Your Word Is Near:* "You are the God of our fathers"
> through "freedom, happiness and peace" on p. 30; the first
> stanza and the last two sentences on p. 31.

FIRST READING:
> Col. 1:15–20.

SECOND READING:
> John 5:19–23.

THE TABLE PRAYER
> "Canon of the Word of God," *The Experimental Liturgy Book,*
> p. 84. People join with celebrant on stanzas beginning "But
> most of all we bless you" and "We recall these words";
> also "So, our Father, may you always be pleased" to the end.

SUGGESTED SONGS:
> All are from *People's Mass Book.*
>
> *Processional:* "Enter, O People of God," #54.
>
> *Procession of Gifts:* "Take Our Bread," #99.
>
> *Communion:* "Like Olive Branches," #159.
>
> *Recessional:* "All You Nations," #142.

A CELEBRATION OF MARRIAGE

OPENING READING:
    1 John 4:11–19.

GREETING

PENITENTIAL RITE:
    "A Wedding Liturgy," *The Experimental Liturgy Book*, p. 142.

FIRST READING:
    "The Song of the Beloved," *Prayers, Poems and Songs*, p. 135.

RESPONSE:
    "Prayer of St. Francis of Assisi," *Discovery in Prayer*, p. 99.

THE GOSPEL:
    Matthew 5:3–16.

EXCHANGE OF WEDDING VOWS

PROFESSION OF FAITH:
    Celebrant: I believe in God, the Father Almighty, Creator of
        heaven and earth . . .
    People: The Father hovering over creation, bursting into the
        world of time and space. I believe in God who is creating,
        now, through men and women at the service of new life
        and growth in that life.
    Celebrant: I believe in Jesus Christ his only Son, our Lord,
        who was conceived by the Holy Spirit, born of the Virgin
        Mary . . .
    People: I believe in Jesus Christ, not only in the Lord of
        history but in the risen Lord who lives today, conceived
        in the washing waters of baptism, who becomes flesh in
        the members of his new body.
    Celebrant: I believe in Jesus Christ, who suffered under
        Pontius Pilate, was crucified, died and was buried; and
        descended into hell;

239

People: I believe in Jesus Christ who is crucified and dying in the suffering of the world today.

Celebrant: The third day, he rose again from the dead. He ascended into heaven.

People: I believe in Jesus Christ who is lifting up the world today through peacemakers.

Celebrant: I believe in Jesus Christ, who sits at the right hand of the Father Almighty, and will come to judge the living and the dead;

People: I believe in Jesus Christ who is coming now, who is judging now, who is building his kingdom now, through the Christian lives of men and women.

Celebrant: I believe in the Holy Spirit, the Holy Catholic Church, the communion of saints, the forgiveness of sins, the resurrection of the body and life everlasting.

People: I believe in the resurrection of the body and life everlasting, in the kingdom being built by Christ in the Spirit through men who are rooting up, tearing down, planting and building the kingdom today for tomorrow's world.

THE TABLE PRAYER

"A Table Prayer for a Wedding Day," *Prayers, Poems, and Songs,* p. 137. People join with celebrant on stanza beginning "You said, 'Let there be light,'" and stanza beginning "Keep them together in love."

SUGGESTED RECESSIONAL:

"Peace, Joy, and Happiness," *Hand in Hand,* #11.

A CELEBRATION OF
A WEDDING ANNIVERSARY

GREETING

PENITENTIAL RITE:
"A Wedding Liturgy," *The Experimental Liturgy Book*, p. 142.
Before the final sentence insert this: "Father, pardon us, and
grant that we may pardon one another."

FIRST READING:
The Song of Songs 2:8–9a, 10–14.

RESPONSE:
1 John 7–11, 12b.

THE GOSPEL:
John 15:9–12.

WEDDING CREED AND VOWS:
"A Wedding Liturgy," *The Experimental Liturgy Book*, p. 143.

THE TABLE PRAYER
"A Table Prayer for a Wedding Day," *Prayers, Poems, and
Songs*, p. 137. People join with celebrant on stanza beginning
"You said, 'Let there be light,'" and stanza beginning "Keep
them together in love."

SUGGESTED SONGS:

Processional: "Enter, O People of God," *People's Mass Book*,
#54.

Procession of Gifts: "All That I Am," *People's Mass Book*, #98.

Communion: "Whatsoever You Do," *People's Mass Book*,
#208.

Recessional: "You Fill the Day," *Hand in Hand*, #4.

THE FEAST OF THE BODY OF CHRIST

GREETING AND PENITENTIAL RITE

FIRST READING:
1 Corinthians 11:23–29.

SECOND READING:
"Prayer over the City," *Prayers for Pagans*, p. 40. Use appropriate slides, if available.

RESPONSE:
Ps. 145:15–16.

THE GOSPEL:
John 6:56–59.

SUGGESTED SONGS:
All are from *People's Mass Book.*

Processional: "All the Earth," #141.

Response to First Reading: "To Be Your Body," refrain only, #131.

Procession of Gifts: "Take Our Bread," #99.

Communion: "Whatsoever You Do," #208.

Recessional: "Prayer for Peace," #205.

A CELEBRATION OF FREEDOM: INDEPENDENCE DAY

GREETING AND **P**ENITENTIAL **R**ITE

GLORIA

PRAYER

FIRST **R**EADING:
Vatican II in *Faces of Freedom*, p. 48.

SECOND **R**EADING:
Galatians 5:13–15.

RESPONSE:
Martin Luther in *Horizons of Hope*, p. 168.

THE **G**OSPEL:
John 8:28–32.

THE TABLE PRAYER
"An American Canon," *The Underground Mass Book*, p. 27.
People join with celebrant on line beginning "We your people"
and continue through next two sentences; also directly after
consecration through "struggle to make them strong"; also
"Through Christ our Lord" to the end.

SUGGESTED **S**ONGS:

Processional: "Come Away," *Hymnal for Young Christians*,
p. 290.

Procession of Gifts: "Prayer for Peace," *People's Mass Book*,
#205.

Communion: "Sons of God," *Hymnal for Young Christians*,
p. 98.

Recessional: "America the Beautiful," *People's Mass Book*,
#231.

A CELEBRATION OF LABOR DAY

GREETING AND PENITENTIAL RITE

PRAYER

FIRST READING:
John Figueroa in *Horizons of Hope*, p. 110.

SECOND READING:
Louis M. Savary in *Horizons of Hope*, p. 123.

RESPONSE:
Romans 12:1.

THE GOSPEL:
Matthew 5:13–16.

THE TABLE PRAYER

"Canon of God's Work," *The Underground Mass Book*, p. 38.
People join with celebrant on second, fourth, and last stanzas.

SUGGESTED SONGS:

Processional: "St. Joseph the Worker," *People's Mass Book*,
#222.

Procession of Gifts: "Of My Hands," *Hymnal for Young
Christians*, p. 79.

Communion: "All the Earth," *People's Mass Book*, #141.

Recessional: "They'll Know We Are Christians by Our Love,"
Hymnal for Young Christians, p. 132.

TWENTY-ONE CONTEMPORARY LITURGIES

Advent and Christmas Themes

Church Unity

Lent and Easter Themes

Pentecost

Trinity

Father's Day

Theme: Sense of Touch

Theme: Ecology

Theme: Independence

Theme: Justice

Theme: Person-to-Person

Five Liturgies on Hope

Each of the liturgies that follow was planned by a committee consisting of the celebrant, the coordinator, and three to seven other interested people who form one of four or five rotating committees. Each celebration is planned around a single, pertinent question which hopefully the congregation will ask themselves during the week following the liturgy. The Service of the Word is so planned that the Gospel or principal Scripture reading and the Homily come, not as a specific answer, but as a significant direction in answering the question.

The Saturday evening Mass which has become our contemporary liturgy began as a "guitar Mass." For this reason nearly all of our selections are appropriate for guitar. Obviously other songs, to be accompanied by the organ and/or other instruments, would be equally effective in conveying the theme.

Mary Sue Greer
Coordinator of Contemporary Liturgy
Christ King Church,
Tulsa, Oklahoma

ADVENT THEME: DREAMS

The general outline of this liturgy and the selection of readings
are taken from "Dreams," An Advent Liturgy, *Children's
Liturgies,* ed. Virginia Sloyan and Gabe Huck (Washington, D.C.:
The Liturgical Conference, 1970). Slides may be used as available
and appropriate, but the narrative is complete without visual
aids. The atmosphere of darkness or semi-darkness, as required for
slides, helps to convey the mood of the liturgy.

First Reader:
   Welcome, Dreamers. All men of all times have been
dreamers; else men would not have survived. The dreams of
the Hebrew people crystallized in a desire for a Messiah.
Like the Hebrew people, we do not hold so tenaciously to
our dreams when we go untouched by poverty, starvation,
disease, or war—as long as we succumb to the illusion that our
wealth of resources will last indefinitely. Realizing our poverty
and that of the world, let us join in our first hymn, "O
Come, O Come Emmanuel," recognizing that the "dream"—
the saving action of the Messiah—must be accomplished
through us.

People:
   "O Come, O Come, Emmanuel!," *People's Mass Book,* #1.

First Reader:
   Night is a time for dreaming; day is a time for making
dreams come true. Men have always dreamed; many blessings
are ours today only because another man dared to dream—and
to work to make his dream come true. We dream most often
and most earnestly when we feel bored, or restricted, or
deprived, or hungry, or cold, or uncomfortable, or lonely.
Some men dream with the loneliness, the desire of the whole
world. Such a man was Isaiah—this was his dream:

Second Reader:
   Isaiah 2:2–4.

First Reader:

> Children too have such dreams. In fact, they are the
> professional dreamers among us.

Third Reader (a child):

> "Last Night I Had the Strangest Dream," *Discovery in Song,*
> p. 110.

People:

> "Peace, My Friends," *Hymnal for Young Christians,* Vol. II,
> p. 34.

First Reader:

> Joachim and Ann were a beautiful couple, steeped in the
> desire, the dream of their people, for a Savior who would
> redeem, would make all things new. Their daughter, Mary,
> shared their dream—and had dreams of her own, which they
> were careful never to bruise or destroy. The greatest dream
> of all came true in Mary. She shared that dream with her
> cousin Elizabeth and with us in a beautiful song of praise
> which we will listen to now. It is like a heart-burst of praise
> for a dream come true.

Choir:

> "Magnificat." A small group should sing this in the most
> beautiful version (chant or part-music) of which they are
> capable. It should be sung in English and enunciated with
> care as this is the Gospel for the day.

First Reader:

> Only a dreamer could have gone—much like a hippie—to
> the desert as John the Baptist did. We don't know exactly
> what happened there, but when John returned to the Jordan
> to get down to business, he spoke the language of a dreamer:

Second Reader:

> Get the Lord's way ready for him.
> Level the mountains, fill up the valleys,
>   straighten the path of the Lord.

First Reader:

But he knew what his dream meant. He was a practical
man with a mandate to make his dream come true. He
explained his dream to those who sincerely inquired, in no
uncertain terms:

Second Reader:

If you have two shirts, give to him who has none;
    whoever has food must share it.
Businessmen, don't overcharge your customers.
Soldiers, policemen, take advantage of no one
    by force or false charges.

First Reader:

The great dream of all times has come true in Jesus—but
like every other dream-come-true, Jesus cannot be pushed
off, imposed on anyone. A dream must rise from within.
Jesus' dream of a world of peace must become our dream:
our imaginations, our hopes, our hands, and feet must make
his dream come true.

This great dream of Jesus Christ comes true all around us
in great novels like *War and Peace* or in architecture—the
Oral Roberts Prayer Tower, for example—in Disneyland
Fantasy and Rodgers and Hammerstein's music; in the
breathtaking vision of Chardin; in the fantastic dream of
John XXIII that has set all of Christendom on a new path;
in the manner of living and dying of people like Martin
Luther King. This great prophet and apostle of non-violence
speaks as the prophets of the Old Testament did for people
poor, deprived, desolate beyond the imagination of all of us
here.

Second Reader or Record:

Martin Luther King's sermon, "I Have a Dream," *My Life
with Martin Luther King, Jr.*, pp. 239–240. This excerpt may
be read or played from an original recording by Martin Luther
King, Jr., if available.

People:

"Hold Fast to Dreams," *Listen to Love*, p. 18.

First Reader:

Do you have a dream to share today? We will have to share
our dream of peace with others if that dream is to come true.
This is true of nearly all our dreams. Perhaps today the best
thing we can do is share our dream of what this contemporary
liturgy can become for us.

A moderator takes over, suggesting that the people divide
into small groups; at end of about four minutes' discussion, reaction
is asked from spokesman from each group. (In all takes 7–8
minutes).

Liturgy resumes with Eucharist. There is no song at
Procession of Gifts, rather time for "dreaming." At Communion
Ed Ames' record of "The Impossible Dream" is played. As
Recessional, all are asked to join in singing with the record.

CHRISTMAS THEME:
A CELEBRATION OF PEACE

INTRODUCTION:

As the Christmas season grows to a close, we ask ourselves
how much real peace this year's celebration of Christmas
has brought to each of us and our families—to our world? Six
weeks have passed since we experienced the fact and fantasies
of Christmas. Do we find in ourselves or in the world around
us any peace left over? any peace that will last? even any
hope for peace? If not, an editor of *The Christian Herald*
suggests the reason why.

FIRST READING:

Excerpts from "Peace Has People In It," *The Christian Herald*,
December 1970, pp. 10–14.

RESPONSE:

Silent reflection

INTRODUCTION TO SECOND READING:

Are we ready to say "Peace on earth, good will to men"
and mean it? If we have illusions about what peace means
in our homes and on our highways, what about peace among
nations? The editor of *Look* magazine suggests that we do
not work for peace (and hence we do not pray for it)
because we really don't want it. If peace were offered us
tomorrow—world peace—we probably would be afraid to
accept it.

SECOND READING:

Excerpts from "Whatever Happened to Mankind's Dream of
Peace?," *Look*, December 29, 1970, pp. 13–17.

RESPONSE:

"Where Have All the Young Men Gone?," from any available
folk collection.

251

THE GOSPEL:

> Matthew 18:19–20. The celebrant briefly comments on the
> Gospel—then allows time for reflection.

RESPONSE:

> Father, your Son has told us plainly
>   that whenever two of us on earth agree
>   about anything we pray for,
>   you will do it for us.
> We do not allow you to answer
>   our prayers for peace
>   because we haven't taken time to understand
>   what "peace on earth" really means;
>   nor have we really agreed to accept that peace,
>   should you offer it to us.
> Grant, Father, that we may be open
>   to peace as it really is,
>   to peace as it is already present among us
>   in your Son, in whose name we pray.

THE TABLE PRAYER:

> "Eucharistic Prayer of Human Unity," *The Experimental
> Liturgy Book*, p. 100.

SUGGESTED SONGS:

> *Processional:* "Prayer for Peace," *People's Mass Book*, #205.
> *Procession of Gifts:* "Take Our Bread," *People's Mass Book*,
>   #99.
> *Communion:* "Let There Be Peace On Earth."
> *Recessional:* "Peace, My Friends," *Hymnal for Young
> Christians*, Vol. II, p. 34.

A CELEBRATION OF CHRISTIAN UNITY

It is appropriate for this celebration of Church unity to ask a minister of another denomination to conduct the Service of the Word.

INTRODUCTION, FIRST READING, AND GOSPEL:
The history of ecumenism and the spirit of the movement (The Gospel) should be excerpted, along with appropriate slides, from the film strip and record, "The Ecumenical Bit" published by Thomas S. Klise Co., Peoria, Illinois. The narrative is done by a minister rather than from the record.

RESPONSE:
The following may be used at an appropriate interval during the reading above and also at the end.
Reader: We were called to be one in the Spirit of God, in the bond of peace.
People: "Priestly People," antiphon only, *People's Mass Book,* #146. This is also repeated after each of the following statements:
Reader: We were called to form one body in one spirit.
Reader: We were called in the same hope in Christ our Lord.
Reader: We were called to be one in the Spirit of God, in the bond of peace.

SUGGESTED SONGS:
Processional: "God Is Love," *Hymnal for Young Christians,* p. 95.
Communion: "They'll Know We Are Christians by Our Love," *Hymnal for Young Christians,* p. 132.
Recessional: "Shout Out Your Joy," *Hymnal for Young Christians,* Vol. II, p. 29.

SUGGESTED PRAYERS:
Last stanza on p. 99 and "Reform your church," p. 147, *Your Word Is Near.*

253

SUNDAY BEFORE ASH WEDNESDAY

Theme: The Same Spirit Gives to Each Man a Different Gift

INTRODUCTION:

At this season when we prepare mutually to observe a
season of preparation, we are tempted to ask the question
posed to Jesus: "Why is it that we and the Pharisees fast
often, but your disciples don't fast at all?" Why is it, we ask
ourselves, that I do one thing to observe Lent while my
neighbor does something different that makes no sense at all
to me? Often we are not even sure that the things we
ourselves choose to do make sense. The answer Jesus gives
in the Gospel today tells us much about the nature of
penance as preparation. He tells us that penance is *for each
one* whatever helps him not only to anticipate the reign of
love and concern but also to precipitate or bring about that
kingdom. One of us may have the gift of fasting; another,
the gift of consoling; another, the gift of preparing liturgies;
another, the gift of good humor; another, the gift of
brightening the world by making beautiful things. The elderly
have a gift of their own; the young, their own—and even the
middle-aged have a very unique gift. That's what today's
liturgy is all about—using our own gift, respecting and
accepting the gifts of others, as all of us together prepare to
accompany the Man of Sorrows through death to resurrection.

FIRST READING:
1 Corinthians 12:4–5, 12–21.

RESPONSE:
"On Giving," *The Prophet,* p. 20. Use stanza beginning
"There are those who give little. . . ."

THE GOSPEL:
Luke 5:33–39.

RESPONSE:

New wine in new wineskins;
old wine in old wineskins.
Let those of us not fast
who understand why we do not fast.
Let those of us fast
who understand why we do.
And let us each respect the integrity of the other.
Nobody who has been drinking old wine wants new—
The old cannot remember the past
too clearly, too painfully.
The young cannot act on experience
they do not have.
But let us each help the other
to find the quality of the grape—
the constant in the new wine as it grows old.
Let the old help the young
find in new wine the promise of the old.
Let the young help the old to remember
when their now-old wine was new
and they drank it
despite the warning of their elders.

FIRST SUNDAY OF LENT

Theme: What Does It Mean To Be a Son of God?

INTRODUCTION:

Last week we said that each of us has a different gift
from the same Spirit and we encouraged one another to use
our unique gifts in the observance of Lent—in *one* Spirit.
This week we would like to talk about the personal freedom
that is necessary if we are to be able to exercise our own
particular talent.

The Gospel provides our focal point. It is the story of the
devil tempting Jesus in the desert: "If you are God's Son,
order these stones to turn into bread. . . . If you are God's
Son, throw yourself to the ground. . . ." The devil asked Christ
to conform to his idea of who the Son of God is and what
he should do. We often play the devil to each other with
such threats as these:

"If you are a loyal citizen, you will not demonstrate in
the streets."

"If you are a real Christian, you will put up with abuses
around you until *authority* does something about them."

"If you weren't a Mama's boy, you'd let your hair grow."

"If you were a good Catholic you wouldn't attend that
five o'clock liturgy unless you absolutely couldn't make it to
Mass the next day."

Thus by our unwarranted and illogical criticism, we ask
others to "defend" their identity (*our* idea of what that identity
ought to be) by rejecting their *real* identity. Our threats
discourage people from being honest, from being courageous
in many of the ways Christ asks his followers to be courageous.

This then is our consideration for today. We would like you
to share some of the thought-provoking things that different
authors have written about the meaning of personal freedom.
But first let us ask forgiveness for some of the ways that
already come to our minds that we have failed to allow others
to exercise their freedom as Sons of God.

PENITENTIAL RITE:
> (*Response:* Lord, have mercy.)
> For imposing our own standards on others and thus keeping
>   them from being honest with themselves; we ask forgiveness,
>   Lord:
> For discouraging others in works of creativity and works of
>   justice by our threatening criticism; we ask forgiveness,
>   Lord:
> For failing to trust that others are as earnest in their search
>   for truth and justice as we think ourselves to be, we ask
>   forgiveness, Lord:

PRAYER

FIRST READING:
> Thomas Merton in *Faces of Freedom*, p. 14. Use introduction
> given on the same page.

RESPONSE:
> George P. Counts in *Faces of Freedom*, p. 26.

SECOND READING:
> Galatians 4:4–7. Introduction: Jesus was unafraid in the face
> of his adversary. He felt no obligation to answer his challenger
> in the terms of the challenge, because he, Jesus, was utterly
> sure of his identity and his freedom as the Son of God.
> Paul acquaints us with the startling fact that we share in the
> identity of Jesus as sons of God:

THE GOSPEL:
> Matthew 4:1–11.

THE TABLE PRAYER:
> "Canon of the Sons of God," *Eucharistic Liturgies*, p. 194.

SUGGESTED PRAYERS:
> *Eucharistic Liturgies*, p. 23–24.

SUGGESTED SONGS:

All are from *Hymnal for Young Christians.*

Processional: "Here We Are," p. 66.

Response to Second Reading: "Bless the Lord," refrain only, p. 71.

Procession with Gifts: "Here We Are," cited above, third, fourth, and fifth verses.

Communion: "Love One Another," p. 81.

Recessional: "Sons of God," p. 98.

A CELEBRATION OF
THE MYSTERY OF WATER

The following Service of the Word can be effectively illustrated with slides available from amateur collections in the parish.

First Reader:

A storm is gathering. Dark blue clouds hover close to the earth. Dry grass seems charged with electric anticipation. Then it happens. One fat, splashy raindrop falls from the heavens, then another and another. If you listen, you might hear a child in the distance singing . . .

People:

(All the people, especially the children are asked to sing this mood song.) "Raindrops Keep Fallin' on My Head."

First Reader:

Few of us have ever had to go as long as a day without water. It is hard for us to imagine the savage thirst that envelops a man deprived of this life-giving substance we so take for granted.

But water means even more than survival for man and all that sustains man—it means the richness of enjoyment and relaxation. Conjure up your own most meaningful experience of water—walking in the rain—or the snow; swimming, float-ing, learning to relax in the arms of something greater than oneself; sailing, water skiing, wading in an icy mountain stream.

In talking with Job, the Lord seeks to impress him with the marvelous things he, Yahweh, has done with water. Perhaps we shall be as impressed as Job was:

Second Reader:

Job 37:5–18.

First Reader:

259

Through the use of water from the earliest times the Lord
has prepared his people for the revelation of baptism. When
the world was first created, the Spirit hovered over the
waters, making them fruitful. The flood that Noah survived
was an image of rebirth—as was the escape of the children
of Abraham through water—the Red Sea. In the water of
the Jordan Jesus was baptized. In his encounter with the
Samaritan woman, he speaks of the torrent of everlasting
water—of divine Sonship—that wells up within him, and that
must be shared:

Celebrant:
John 4:5–30, 39–42.

SUGGESTED SONG FOR PROCESSION OF GIFTS
AND/OR RECESSIONAL:
"Amazing Grace," Traditional.

EASTER THEME:
SHARING THE RESURRECTION

INTRODUCTION:

    If you have ever been the bearer of earth-shaking good news, you will appreciate the feelings of Mary Magdalene as she ran to tell the apostles that Christ had risen. In some sense the resurrection had become not only the Father's gift to the world but hers as well. And so it seems that from the moment of his rising, Jesus was sharing, and asking others to share, the wonder, the joy, and the support-to-faith that resurrection is.

    Today Jesus shares resurrection with his disciples as they are fishing—giving new meaning by his presence to their fantastic haul of fish and to the appetizing breakfast he has prepared for them.

    A passage from the French classic, *The Little Prince,* is our first reading. In it the Little Prince explains that the water offered him by his friend is like no other water in the world because of the bond of friendship that exists between them. These few paragraphs crystallize the openness-to-another that makes it possible for us to share the meaning and hope of resurrection with others even as Jesus in today's liturgy shares it with us.

FIRST READING:

    Chapter 25, *The Little Prince,* from the beginning of the chapter through "One must look with the heart."

RESPONSE:

    Paragraph beginning "The believer is a man. . . ." p. 35, *Prayers, Poems, and Songs.*

THE GOSPEL:

    John 21:1–14.

THE TABLE PRAYER:

    "Canon of the New Creation," *The Underground Mass Book,* p. 24.

SUGGESTED SONGS:

Processional: "Gonna Sing, My Lord," *People's Mass Book,* #201.

Communion: "Sing Out, My Soul, to the Lord," *Come Alive,* p. 27.

Recessional: "Allelu!," *Hymnal for Young Christians,* p. 126.

EASTER THEME:
WE TOO ARE SHEPHERDS

INTRODUCTION:

Just as Jesus left us the "Our Father" not only as a prayer but as a *way* to pray, so he has left us the parables, not just as a gift in themselves, but as a way to think. As we look at each of his parables, we are asked to bring from our treasure of faith and imagination old things and new. With reverence for all that has been, we must seek still newer meanings for each parable, more relevant symbols and names by which to comprehend what Jesus is really saying to us.

So it is that in preparing for this—Good Shepherd Sunday —the committee sought terms by which to better understand the fullness of the pastoral allegories. We concluded that the nearest equivalent we could find in our own times and culture for the term "shepherd" is *one who cares*—one who cares to the extent of giving his life daily for his fellow man as, for example, our politicians are asked to do—or, of giving it all at once, as (*use example currently meaningful to the congregation*). We also concluded that, in reading the gospel of the Good Shepherd, we are to identify not just with the sheep, *the cared for*, but with the shepherd, the *one who cares* —as father, mother, brother or sister, teacher, as representative of others in the civic or social order, as members of the healing professions, as postmen, garbage collectors, grocery men—or just as fellow human beings.

FIRST READING:

"Secret in His Dying," *Wonder and Worship*, p. 79. This story may be read as is, shortened, or told in the reader's own words. Previous to the celebration, a group of children may be asked to listen to the story and then draw in crayons or paint their reaction to the story. By means of an opaque projector, their art work may be used to illustrate the story as it is being told during the liturgy.

RESPONSE:

After a minute or so of silent reflection, the reader reads current headlines dealing with tragedies and with people who care. The people respond to each with "We too are called to be shepherds of men."

THE GOSPEL:

John 10:11–18.

THE TABLE PRAYER:

"Dutch Canon," *The Experimental Liturgy Book*, p. 46.

SUGGESTED SONGS:

All are from *Hymnal for Young Christians*, Vol. II.
Processional: "I Am The Resurrection," p. 28.
Procession of Gifts: "And I Will Follow," p. 122.
Recessional: "Allelu," p. 32.
During Communion it is appropriate to read "Of Pain," *The Prophet*, p. 47.

A CELEBRATION OF PENTECOST

Theme: "In One Spirit We Are All Baptized, Making One Body"

INTRODUCTION:
Informal introduction of theme by celebrant.

FIRST READING:
Acts 2:1–11, read simultaneously in eight different languages by eight different readers standing in different parts of the church. The reader at the microphone is reading in English. All readers "resolve" into English on line, "we hear them preaching in our own language."

RESPONSE:
"Peace, My Friends," *Hymnal for Young Christians*, Vol. II, p. 34.

THE GOSPEL:
John 20:19–23.

BAPTISM:
The sacrament is administered in the sanctuary so that all may see. If person being baptized is an infant or child, the people then sing Carey Landry's "Song of Baptism" to welcome the child. This is sung as the gifts are brought to the altar.

THE PREFACE:
"Unity Preface," *The Experimental Liturgy Book*, p. 27.

SUGGESTED SONGS:
All are from *Yes, The Spirit Is A-Movin'*.
Processional and Recessional: "The Spirit Is A-Movin'," #1.
Procession of Gifts: (If child is baptized) "Song of Baptism," #17.
Communion: "Lord, You Love," #26.

A CELEBRATION OF TRINITY

Theme: "By the Spirit's Power We Cry to God, 'Father, My Father.'"

INTRODUCTION:

This is Trinity Sunday, fittingly placed just after Pentecost, as a time for celebrating the three-in-oneness or community in God, as it is reflected in the community of men. As we are reminded by Vatican II (here read from Vatican II, p. 78, in *Listen to Love*).

It is the renewing Spirit who unites Father and Son, and who unites us with one another. In this unity of the Spirit Paul invites us to find hope. (Here read Romans 8:14–17.)

FIRST READING:

Our first reading is an excerpt from Diane Pike's story of her search for help the night after she and her husband found themselves stranded in the desert. She forces herself to concentrate on the hope of finding another human being in the wilderness—one who will mean the difference between life and death to her. She finally hears the answer of the Spirit in the "Shalom" of an Arab construction worker. "The Desert Ordeal of Bishop Pike," an excerpt from *Search*, in *Ladies Home Journal*, January 1970. Read page 109 from "It was now about 2:30 in the morning . . ." to the end.

RESPONSE:

"You are the breath and the fire," Huub Oosterhuis, *Your Word Is Near*, p. 107. The entire page may be used or excerpts from it. As a reminder of the Spirit-in-community, the lines may be divided and marked on the program to be read by women, men, boys, and girls, respectively.

THE GOSPEL:

John 16:12–15.

THE PREFACE:

266

"Unity Preface," *The Experimental Liturgy Book,* p. 27.

SUGGESTED SONGS:
   Processional: "Bless the Lord," *Hymnal for Young Christians,*
      p. 71.
   Procession of Gifts: "They'll Know We Are Christians by Our
      Love," *Hymnal for Young Christians,* p. 132.
   Communion: "Let There Be Peace on Earth."
   Recessional: "Shalom," *Hymns for Now I.* This most
      appropriately suggests the interaction of community, if
      sung as a round.

A CELEBRATION OF FATHER'S DAY

INTRODUCTION:
> None today; theme should be set in Greeting and Prayer of Invocation.

FIRST READING:
> "Dumb Giant Tom," *Wonder and Worship*, p. 87. This can be done effectively with three readers: narrator, Tom, and a third reader to take remaining parts; the story should be abbreviated to emphasize Tom's search for a father.

RESPONSE:
> Silent reflection.

THE GOSPEL:
> Luke 15:11–32. List on program as "A Parable of a Father's Love."

THE TABLE PRAYER:
> "Canon of the New Creation," *The Underground Mass Book*, p. 24.

SUGGESTED SONGS:
> *Processional:* "The Spirit Is A-Movin'," *Yes, the Spirit Is A-Movin'*, #1.
> *Procession of Gifts:* "God the Father, Hear Our Prayer," *Hymnal for Young Christians*, p. 4. Use refrain as response to General Intentions, sung or spoken by celebrant.
> *Communion:* "Let There Be Peace On Earth."
> *Recessional:* "We Long For You, O Lord," *Hymnal for Young Christians*, p. 90. Use "Father, Son, and Holy Spirit . . ." as refrain.

A CELEBRATION OF
THE SENSE OF TOUCH

INTRODUCTION:
"Some Sight of God," *A New Catechism,* p. 253, to the
end of page.

FIRST READING:
Our first reading today consists of a summary in our own
words of the things we learned about the significance of touch
as we prepared for today's liturgy.

We discovered, first of all, that the concordance we were
using lists 28 references to the word "touch" in the Old
Testament. Each of the 28 references is negative. Always
there is the admonition "Touch not this or touch not that"
or the prayer that one would not be touched in a harmful
way. By contrast there are seven references to "touch" in
the Gospels, six of which are positive. Crowds or individuals
reach out to touch Jesus—or even the hem of his garment.
It is as though a people ruled by fear and restriction and
tending to withdraw into themselves suddenly discover that
touch is a positive power that can put them in contact with
the greatest conceivable living good.

We considered then our own times—the hundreds of "Look
but do not touch" signs we have all read; the caution to
children to say "excuse me" if they accidentally brush against
someone; the tendency of industrialization to keep us from
the feel of the soil, of raw food, of the raw materials we work
with; the prevalence of air conditioning and heating systems
which insulate us from the temperature changes of the seasons.
We too are a "touch not" generation.

We turned then to science and psychology, which tell us
these things about the significance of touch: Ashley Montagu
questioned why certain mammals lick the skin of their
young immediately after birth, and found that this was not
a method of cleansing but the first movement in a
communication process through the skin and its nerve
beginnings. He discovered that unlicked animals do not

269

survive because certain physiological systems, which should have been alerted by stimulation, are never roused to action.

Psychologists tell us that the closeness to his mother felt by a baby while he is being nursed is as important as the food he is receiving. The fondling of an infant is more than the mere stroking of the skin; it is the stimulation of sources of energy and a communication of life. In a recent talk, Margaret Mead asserted that whether a child is breast-fed or bottle-fed, the closeness to his mother's body, especially at feeding time, in some mysterious way "teaches" a child that he is a human being. On the negative side we learned that people who have an inordinate fear of touching or being touched are emotionally unstable, if not mentally ill.

All this brought us to realize, with a new sense of gratitude, what was read in our call to worship today. God the Father in Jesus—and Jesus in the Church—and now his own Spirit in us—constantly reach out to touch us, to assure us of the goodness of all touchable things, and of the power of touch to communicate life, to assure us of our very real need to be in *touch* with each other. The gesture of forgiveness, of anointing, of pouring water, of offering food—through our sense of touch we perceive these gestures and understand that God loves us very much.

(Of special value in this study was the chapter, "Sight and Touch," *A Theology of Things*. The quote by Edwin Brock on page 54 of this book so effectively conveys the "feel" of this liturgy that it should be printed on the program for meditation.)

RESPONSE:
We thank you, Father, for all our senses,
    but especially today for the gift of touch.
We thank you for heat and for cold,
    for sun tans, swimming, and skiing.
We thank you for the feel of cool water, hot coffee,
    for icy cokes and warm bread.
We thank you for the velvet of rose petals,
    the prickle of cactus,

the scratch of grass on bare legs,
the feel of soil in our hands.
We thank you for cats and dogs—
for sleekness and curliness
and a cold nose in our hands;
for the flying mane of a horse
and his quick response to the touch of a rein.
We thank you for the coolness of our mother's hand
on a feverish head;
the strength in our father's arms;
the tug of a child's hand in ours.
We thank you, Father, for all the gentleness and strength
husbands and wives can find in each other's arms.
We thank you, Father, for touching us in all these ways,
but above all for touching us in your Son Jesus
as he walked the roads of Galilee
and as he now walks our streets.
We thank you for the gestures, the movement,
thy physical contact that make the sacraments
your continuing way of touching us—
through your priests and through one another.
Let us ever feel the touch of your hand!

THE GOSPEL:
Luke 8:43–48.

THE TABLE PRAYER:
"Eucharistic Prayer by John C. L'Heureux," *The Experimental Liturgy Book,* p. 97.

SUGGESTED SONGS:
Processional: "Bless the Lord," *Hymnal for Young Christians,*
p. 71.
Procession of Gifts and Recessional: "Lord, You Live," *Yes, the Spirit Is A-Movin',* #1
Communion: "Peace, My Friends," *Hymnal for Young Christians,* Vol. II, p. 34.

A CELEBRATION OF ECOLOGY

INTRODUCTION:
Informal presentation of theme by celebrant.

FIRST READING:
In your local library find a tale from American Indian lore showing the intimate relation between the Indian and all of nature.

RESPONSE:
Roy Campbell quoted in *A Theology of Things*, p. 11.

PREFACE:
Matthew 25:1–13.

RESPONSE:
Father, we do not know why
  the five foolish virgins had no oil;
  we only know that they had a choice
  of being prepared or not being prepared;
  of being far-sighted or short-sighted.
Father, the "oil" of our universe is running low.
As yet, we still have the choice of providing
  or not providing for generations to come.
We commit ourselves today to active concern
  for the future of the world you have made ours.
May we become one with your Spirit·
  who is constantly renewing the face of the earth.

PREFACE:
"Unity Preface," *The Experimental Liturgy Book*, p. 27.

SUGGESTED SONGS:
Processional: "Rejoice, the Lord Is King," *Hymnal for Young Christians*, p. 115.
Procession of Gifts: "Wonder-Full World," *Hymnal for Young Christians*, p. 266.

Communion: "Put Your Hand in the Hand."
Recessional: "Bless the Lord," *Hymnal for Young Christians,*
   p. 71.

The theme, simply expressed in the Indian proverb, "The
frog does not drink up the pond in which he lives," lends
itself to design in an attractive banner and/or "souvenir"
sheets for members of the congregation to take home.

A CELEBRATION OF INDEPENDENCE

INTRODUCTION:

None today; theme should be set in Greeting and Prayer of Invocation.

FIRST READING:

All read together "The Declaration of Independence."

RESPONSE:

These three statements are read by the reader only; the people respond by singing the lines "All we are saying . . ." to the melody used in the movie, *The Strawberry Statement.*

We hold it to be self-evident that all men are endowed by their creator with these inalienable rights: life, liberty, and the pursuit of happiness.
ALL WE ARE SAYING IS, GIVE HOPE A CHANCE.

In this year of 1971 we find it evident that many United States' citizens are deprived of their right to speak and be heard; to gain, and be recognized for, personal competence; to live freely in a self-chosen way of life.
ALL WE ARE SAYING IS, GIVE MEN A CHANCE.

We hold that whenever any form of government becomes destructive of these rights or inadequate in providing them for all, *it is time for a revolution in the hearts of men.*
ALL WE ARE SAYING IS, GIVE LIFE A CHANCE.

THE GOSPEL:
John 2:13–22.

RESPONSE:

To each of the following petitions, read by the celebrant, the people answer, "It is time for a revolution in the hearts of men."
Lord, you demanded for your Father the respect you demand for each of us; lead us in revolt against our own prejudices, by which we deprive each other of that respect.

274

Lord, you revolted against man's commercializing of religion, creating of it a bureaucracy for the benefit of a few; lead us in revolt against our own apathy—which has allowed both government and Church to fall prey to the abuses of bureaucracy.

Lord, you revolted against every kind of discrimination—sex, race, creed, alleged innocence or alleged guilt; lead us in revolt against our stubborn determination *not to see* the real plight of our suffering fellow men, whom we claim this day to be entitled to life, liberty, and the pursuit of happiness.

THE TABLE PRAYER:

"Canon for a Day of Thanksgiving," *Eucharistic Liturgies*, p. 199.

SUGGESTED SONGS:

Processional: "This Land Is Your Land," *124 Folk Songs*, p. 100.

Procession of Gifts: Melody as in "Let Us Break Bread Together," *Hymnal for Young Christians*, p. 89. Words as follows:

Hear the good news, my brothers, Christ is peace!
Hear the good news, my sisters, Christ is peace!
It is time to restore to each man his own dignity
And live as brothers in peace.
Let us break bread together in his name.
Let us break bread together in his name.
For we share in the life of the one who has died
That we may live as brothers in peace.

Communion: "This Land Is Your Land," cited above, can be used as a humming background for the reading: Section 16, "Song of Myself," Walt Whitman, in any edition of Whitman's work. Read through "Prisoner, fancy-man, rowdy, lawyer, physician, priest." As a conclusion, add last line from preceding section (15).

Recessional: "The Times They Are A-Changing"; use any available version, preferably one which begins, "Come gather round, people, wherever you roam."

A CELEBRATION OF JUSTICE

INTRODUCTION:

INTRODUCTION:
   Celebrant should set the theme, speaking four to five minutes
   on the Gospel, emphasizing that the Good Samaritan was
   doing an act, not of charity, but of justice; and that we tend
   to do acts of charity to relieve our consciences for not
   doing the basic acts of justice—correcting a system which
   makes "acts of charity" necessary. See first reading.

FIRST READING:
   Martin Luther King in *Horizons of Hope*, p. 84.

RESPONSE:
   Solo to be sung during period of reflection. It should be pointed
   out that Martin Luther King (*first reading*) used the words
   of this song to sum up his own attitude toward life and death:
   "If I Can Help Somebody."

THE GOSPEL:
   Luke 10:25–37.

RESPONSE:
   Lord Jesus, you make it clear
      that every man is our neighbor;
      we have piously accepted this in theory
      for as long as we have called ourselves Christian.
   Like the priest and the levite in your story,
      we piously help the poor
      when it suits our purposes—
      making our record look good;
      when it doesn't require that we identify
      with the poor man, person to person,
      and accept the fulfillment of his needs
      as a matter of justice.
   Grant us the patience and generosity
      to continue the work of the Good Samaritan—
      for the right reasons.

276

But, above all, awaken in us the sense of justice
   that will make us politically active
   in correcting structural abuses
   that spawn beggars and secure a caste system.

THE TABLE PRAYER:
   "Eucharistic Prayer of Human Unity," *The Experimental
   Liturgy Book*, p. 100. In the second sentence of the preface,
   after "your gift of love," add, "and of justice."

SUGGESTED SONGS:
   Processional: "Hear, O Lord," *Hymnal for Young Christians*,
      p. 78.
   Offertory: "Take Our Bread," *People's Mass Book*, #99.
   Communion: "Whatsoever You Do," *People's Mass Book*,
      #208.
   Recessional: "We Shall Overcome," first three verses, *Hymnal
   for Young Christians*, p. 300.

A CELEBRATION OF PERSON-TO-PERSON

All references in this liturgy are to *Your Word Is Near.*

INTRODUCTION:
This week's Gospel—the story of Mary and Martha—is a familiar one. There are probably as many interpretations of this story as there are women who have worked in the kitchen wondering when someone would stop visiting long enough to help—or, on the other hand, women who have scolded themselves for being so intent on making something special for a guest that they never have time to enjoy the guest when he arrives. There are those who are not convinced that Martha's role is less meritorious than Mary's and those who think that Mary should have helped Martha precisely so that Martha could more easily have shared in the better part. But no one argues the basic point: the ultimate reason for all kitchen work and house work is the care and nurturing of persons and their enjoyment of each other.

This poses several questions: Do we place persons over things? Do we take time to enjoy the persons in our own family? Do we take time to allow God to become a person in our lives? Do we have the courage to let him become more than a theological definition or a philosophical speculation? Do we ever dare to say, "You, God, yes, I mean you!"

Huub Oosterhuis, a prayerful man from Holland, has some important things to say about prayer in our first reading:

FIRST READING:
This should consist of that part of the "Introduction" to *Your Word Is Near* which is most meaningful to those preparing the liturgy. Excerpts from pages 6, 7, 2, 3, 12 (*in that order*) were used in the original liturgy.

RESPONSE:
"How many times, God, have we been told that you are no stranger," p. 19.

THE GOSPEL:
Luke 10:38–42.

RESPONSE:
Silent reflection.

THE TABLE PRAYER:
"The Great Prayer of Thanksgiving," *Your Word Is Near*,
p. 114.

SUGGESTED PRAYERS OF INVOCATION AND BENEDICTION:
"God, this word we call you by," p. 57; "God, we break
bread for one another," p. 121.

SUGGESTED SONGS:
All are from *Hymnal for Young Christians*.
Processional: "Allelu," p. 32.
Procession of Gifts: "God the Father, Hear Our Prayer," p. 96.
Communion: "And I will Follow," p. 122.
Recessional: "Wonder-Full World," p. 109.

FIVE LITURGIES ON THE THEME OF HOPE

In the study and discussion from which the following
liturgies evolved, the committee and coordinator found most
helpful a series of unpublished retreat lectures by Rev. Amandus
di Vincenzo, O.S.B.; *Voices: The Art and Science of Psychotherapy,*
Winter 1970, an issue devoted entirely to the subject of "hope";
A Theology of Things by Conrad Bonifazi; *The Secular City* by
Harvey Cox.

SUGGESTED TABLE PRAYERS:
> "Canon of Christian Hope," *The Experimental Liturgy Book,*
> p. 71.
> "Canon of the New Creation," *The Underground Mass Book,*
> p. 24.

SUGGESTED SONGS FOR LITURGIES ON "HOPE":
> All are from *Hymnal for Young Christians,* Vol. II.
> "And I Will Follow," p. 122.
> "I Am The Resurrection and the Life," p. 28.
> "Wonder-full World," p. 109.
> "We Long For You, O Lord," p. 12.
> "Allelu," p. 32.
> "Hear, O Lord," p. 125.
> "Look Beyond," p. 9.
> "Shout From the Highest Mountain," p. 138.
> "Love One Another," p. 10.
> "Shout Out Your Joy," p. 29.

A CELEBRATION OF THINGS
TO BE HOPED FOR

INTRODUCTION:

Our theme today is "What do we hope for?" If we are
heirs with Jesus Christ, what do we look for as our part of
his inheritance? Let us read together the passage in which
Paul assures us of the nature of our inheritance—of things
we may confidently hope for: (Here all read Romans 8:14–17.)

Until recently our theology of hope has centered on life
after death, looking upon the things of this world as neutral—
to be merely used, tolerated, or even avoided. The Church
now is alive with a new sense of hope. We are taking seriously
the words of St. Paul: "For anyone who is in Christ, there
is a new creation: the old creation has already gone" (2
Cor. 5:17). The Christian sees himself, all other men, and the
universe itself in a state of becoming. The greatest thing a
man can hope for is to become actively a part of this
transformation of which life-beyond-death is simply the
culmination. We will look more closely at several of these
ideas in the weeks ahead. For today, we will ask simply
"What do we hope for? And what values do we look for
and obtain as a result of that hope?"

FIRST READING:

Harvey Cox in *Horizons of Hope*, p. 19.

RESPONSE:

Silent reflection.

SECOND READING:

Romans 8:18–27.

RESPONSE:

This prayer-response is read by the celebrant; the people
respond by singing the lines "All we are saying . . ." to the
melody used in the movie, *The Strawberry Statement.*

Father, the whole of creation is eagerly waiting for us to

281

enter into our inheritance as your children, that we might
truly care for the earth and all living things. Give us the
hope we need to accept the terrible and responsible freedom
that belongs to your sons and daughters.
ALL WE ARE SAYING IS, GIVE LIFE A CHANCE.

Your Son Paul tells us that the whole of creation—and we
in particular—are in the process of one great act of giving
birth. Grant us the trust to accept suffering that has already
become a fact and make it redemptive in your name.
Grant us the hope we need to commit ourselves to removing
the causes of future suffering.
ALL WE ARE SAYING IS, GIVE MEN A CHANCE.

Father, grant us the hope we need to accept realistically
the presence of evil around us but *not* to resign ourselves
to it—rather to actively commit all the years of our lives
to making life bearable, even enjoyable, for those who are
now forgotten, discriminated against, plagued by suffering
and disease, and deprived of any witness to hope in their
fellow man.
ALL WE ARE SAYING IS, GIVE HOPE A CHANCE.

A CELEBRATION OF MAN,
THE HOPE OF THE UNIVERSE

INTRODUCTION:

In some mysterious way, man bears within himself the dynamism of the whole universe. In the Genesis account of creation, God makes man responsible for animals, plants, all the earth. When man proved irresponsible, God cleansed the earth, making a covenant with Noah, reminding man that he must be faithful to the earth, building it and caring for it. Many years later St. Paul insists that all nature is to share in the freedom and glory of the sons of God.

St. Francis of Assisi is one of the great men of all times because he knew what it meant to interact with all nature—with respect and with joy. All through the ages poets have insisted that man is dependent on the earth for life and the enjoyment of life and that nature in turn depends on man for its fuller meaning and value. In our times it is not just the artists and the poets but the scientists as well, such as Teilhard de Chardin and Loren Eiseley, who insist with urgency that man is largely responsible for his own future and the future of the universe. Our first reading is an account from the life of Loren Eiseley, a well-known anthropologist and educator.

FIRST READING:

The story of the "Star-Thrower," pp. 67–92, *The Unexpected Universe,* abbreviated and told in the reader's own words.

RESPONSE:

Silent reflection—what hope does the universe find in me?

SECOND READING:

Romans 8:19–25, 28–29.

RESPONSE:

Same as Response to Second Reading in preceding liturgy.

283

SUGGESTED READING DURING COMMUNION:

"We bring the sun from the distances of space . . ." through "The patient watchers gaze into space, waiting, wondering" (Alastair Reid, *To Be Alive*).

A CELEBRATION OF CHRIST, OUR HOPE

INTRODUCTION:
In Old Testament times as well as in New, God has given his people much cause for hope. For some, the miracle of life itself was reason enough for hope—the mystery of life in all its forms, in all its seasons—the mystery of life through the death of a seed, the mystery of human growth through suffering.

On the other hand, early peoples saw around them, even as we see today, great cause for hopelessness: man's own weakness—even malice, his readiness for lust and for war, the turbulence of nature. In the face of such contradiction, God spoke to one people, the Israelites; he spoke in every image human language could afford, assuring them that, like a loving father, like a faithful spouse or forgiving friend, he would always welcome his people back. More than this, through the voice of Isaiah, the Lord told his people of one who would shoulder their weakness, their guilt. Even as God would have men trust themselves to him, so he would "trust" his Son to men.

FIRST READING:
Isaiah 53:2b–7.

RESPONSE:
Isaiah 55:6–9.

SECOND READING:
Isaiah 54:1–10 or (*shorter*) Isaiah 54:6–10. Celebrant should introduce this briefly with reference to the "spouse" imagery.

SUGGESTED READING DURING COMMUNION:
Excerpts from "Hope," *God Speaks.*

285

A CELEBRATION:
SEEING "FACE TO FACE"

INTRODUCTION:

Today our theme is hope as related to love. The relation between the two is very simple—and essential. We can grow in love only by opening ourselves to another, by being vulnerable, taking the risk of knowing and being known. We have the courage to take this risk only when we have hope—hope of growing in love to a new level of understanding and sensitivity. Rollo May, the author of *Love and Will*, points out that even as two people grow in love, they suffer from the realization that, in this life at least, their union is never complete. So loving and hoping lead two people to the further hope—beyond life as we now know it—of seeing each other "face to face" as Paul puts it in his epistle.

The festival of the assumption is our way of celebrating the life of a woman who loved and hoped above all others. It was hope that led Mary not just to resign herself to the theoretical will of God but to actively, joyfully accept her role as a way of growing in love. We are not interested in the spatial relations implied by the word "assumption"—a going up. What we are interested in and encouraged by is the reality of the assumption—the assurance that Mary sees and enjoys and that we, in turn, will see and will enjoy, "face to face" the Lord of Love, and in him all our loved ones. We will become fully REAL.

Margery Williams in *The Velveteen Rabbit* expresses these profound truths in a simple language—the language of two toy animals talking to each other:

FIRST READING:

"What is REAL?," *The Velveteen Rabbit*, pp. 16–17; from "What is REAL . . ." through "except to people who don't understand."

RESPONSE:

Silent reflection.

SECOND READING:
1 Corinthians 13:4–13.

RESPONSE:
"On Love," *The Prophet*, pp. 13–14. Use stanza beginning "Like sheaves of corn. . . ."

SUGGESTED READING DURING COMMUNION:
"The Love That Is Forever," *Whitman*, pp. 117–118.

A CELEBRATION:
WITNESSES TO HOPE

INTRODUCTION:

A recent issue of *Voices*, a journal of psychotherapy, was devoted entirely to the subject of hope. A number of authors —all of them psychologists or psychiatrists—warned of the danger of giving false hope to a patient. There is a difference, they point out, between a "Pollyanna" attitude which looks unrealistically at the present and the future—and the hope that flows from a sense of actual growth or productivity.

We grow and help others to grow in hope when we and they accept the present realistically—regardless of how painful that may be—and set about working with them for a better future. St. James warns us of the hypocrisy of saying to a man, "You blacks will just have to be patient—things will work out in time" or "Pull yourself up by your own bootstraps" while doing nothing to secure equal rights or provide equal educational opportunities for him and for his children. St. James writes: (Here read James 2:14–16.)

We think St. James would say the same thing of hope— that hope without good works is dead. The man who is not willing to back up his hope with works of justice and charity gives no hope at all—in fact, he has no real hope.

Perhaps never in the history of mankind has it been so difficult to be hopeful about our world, because never before have we been able to see and hear during a 30-minute telecast the state of the world, its agonies as well as its glories. It is difficult to be realistically hopeful about a problem of a size and complexity never known before—we simply are not sure that a solution is possible.

In our first reading, Harvey Cox, one of the great theologians of our times, has an answer for our doubts.

FIRST READING:

Harvey Cox in *Listen to Love*, p. 227.

RESPONSE:

Silent reflection.

THE GOSPEL:

Luke 16:1–8. Introduction: It is not enough for the man of hope to have good intentions or merely be a well-wisher. Now, as never before, he must be energetic, creative, even clever. This brings us to our Gospel—the story of the crafty steward.

RESPONSE:

Father, the children of light are still often
   outdone by the children of darkness.
We are often lazy and unimaginative,
   or paralyzed by fear and pessimism.
Fill us with hope that we may be energetic
   and creative in solving
   the mammoth problems of our times—
   whether it be a problem of changing
   from a wartime to a peacetime economy,
   or of fighting corruption in government,
   or of breaking a racial caste system—
   or a personal problem that at this moment
   seems bigger than all these
   to some member of our families.

FUNERAL LITURGY 1

THE ENTRANCE RITE

INVITATION TO WORSHIP:
There is good news in the midst of all the confusion and
anguish of these last few days; and to proclaim that news
loudly and clearly for all to hear is why we are gathered
together. For Christian men and women, there is no death
except that of Baptism; and they console one another in faith
with that belief—that life is not taken away, it is merely
changed. The best news of all is that in Christ mankind has
experience of this change. It is not promise to be fulfilled; it
has already happened. It is in this spirit of faith that we meet
to break open the word of God for light and wisdom, and
we break bread together for strength and unity. We make a
sign of that unity by our song.

PROCESSIONAL:
"My Soul Is Thirsting" (Ps. 41), *Twenty-Four-Psalms and a
Canticle,* p. 16.

GREETING OF THE BODY OF THE DECEASED AT THE CHURCH DOOR:
Welcome, Christian servant, by these waters of holy Baptism
you were finally freed from all selfishness and sin. You passed
over from your old self to share in the promise of the new
creation in the Kingdom of God. You were nourished on the
bread of life at the table in this place. Sharing in the Passover
of the New Covenant, you are one of God's own people.
We who remain are comforted by this belief, and we turn to the
Gospel of Jesus Christ: (Here read Mark 16:1–8.) This is the
Gospel of Jesus Christ. There is no panic among us today.
We've come here to tell everyone that Jesus is risen and so are
all those who believe in him.
(*The procession enters the church and the singing of Psalm 41
continues.*)

GREETING:

> Christ has died; Christ has risen; Christ will come again.
> May the Spirit of the risen, triumphant Christ be with you all.

PRAYER OF INVOCATION:

> Our Father, we come to you in joy for your favor
> > of unending life made known in Christ Jesus.
> In him all persons and all things are filled with spirit
> > and poured out over our world.
> As you glorified and approved the life of your Son,
> > so now we ask that you remember your servant (*name*),
> > who at this table made himself one with him.
> Sharing the faith by which he held on to you,
> > we give you praise and thanksgiving,
> > today and every day, forever and ever.

THE SERVICE OF THE WORD

FIRST READING:

> Lamentations 3:17–26.

RESPONSE:

> "My Soul Is Longing" (Ps. 130), *Biblical Hymns and Psalms,*
> p. 98.

SECOND READING:

> Revelation 22:1–5; 21:1–4; 22:16–17 (*read without
> interruption*).

GOSPEL ACCLAMATION:

> "Let Hymns of Joy," *Our Parish Prays and Sings,* #83.

THE GOSPEL:

> John 12:23–26.

HOMILY

GENERAL INTENTIONS:

Priest: Let us ask the all-powerful God who raised Jesus from the dead to lift us from the death of these days and this sadness:
    Father in heaven, let us walk in the newness of life,
who were buried through Baptism in the death of your Son
and restored in his resurrection,

All: . . . so that when death overwhelms us, we may be alive always in Christ.

Priest: Give us always the bread of angels to eat, the living bread from heaven,

All: . . . that we may have eternal life and arise on the last day.

Priest: Christ Jesus, comforter of grief-stricken people, you were so moved by the death of Lazarus and by the grief of the widow at Naim and the daughter of the chief of the synagogue, that you compassionately removed the sorrow of relatives and neighbors.

All: Console all who mourn for their dead.

Priest: In your divine plan you permit the destruction of our earthly home.

All: Provide then a home, not made of time, but built of eternity in heaven.

PROCESSIONAL:
    "Let Hymns of Joy," *Our Parish Prays and Sings*, #83, verse 2.

PRAYER OF BLESSING OVER GIFTS:
    "Pray, brothers, that my gift and yours . . ."

THE TABLE PRAYER

PREFACE:
    Father, to you be all praise and thanksgiving.
    We speak on this day of the wonders you perform;
        we praise you for raising to life
        your son and our brother, Jesus.
    He has become the new Adam, born of the earth,
        broken at the hands of men, yet as the grain of wheat
        dying to bring a rich harvest,
        he has disarmed death and mourning and suffering,
        so that their sting does not last forever.

On this day, he becomes the song on every tongue,
   the Word shared among us.
   the Word we shall go on speaking and meeting
   all of our lives so that your faithfulness to us
   is known among our children forever.
We gather around this table then
   in doubt, in love, in risk, in hope,
   to offer you thanks in a new way.
God-touched and frail, yet possessing
   a dignity beautiful beyond belief,
   we strain with all of creation
   to burst the bonds of death
   and with all of your faithful
   rising from their old selves,
   we praise you singing together.

HYMN OF PRAISE:
   "Holy, Holy, Holy," *People's Mass Book,* #106.

ACCLAMATION AT CONSECRATION:
   #139b, *People's Mass Book.*

ENDING ACCLAMATION:
   "Keep in Mind," *People's Mass Book,* #145.

THE SERVICE OF COMMUNION

THE "OUR FATHER"

RITE OF PEACE

SONG:
   None today.

PERIOD OF REFLECTION:
   Intermission

THE DISMISSAL RITE

PRAYER OF BENEDICTION:

   (*All are invited to pray together.*)
   "We pray that nothing" through "to be faithful to us in death,"
   Your Word Is Near, pp. 78–79.

DISMISSAL:

   Prayer beginning on last line, p. 157 of *The Experimental
   Liturgy Book* through the Blessing on p. 158.

RECESSIONAL:

   "Yes, I Shall Arise," *People's Mass Book*, #174.

AT THE CEMETERY

All: Psalm 56:9b–13; Psalm 27:1, 4, 13–14.

Priest: "Our brother has fallen asleep" through "shall appear in his
   glory," *The Experimental Liturgy Book*, pp. 155–156.

DISMISSAL:

   Let us go now in peace and take with us the memory of
   (*name*). We let him go out of our keeping and place him
   in the care of the living God, in the name of the Father
   and of the Son and of the Holy Spirit. Amen.

FUNERAL LITURGY 2

THE ENTRANCE RITE

INVITATION TO WORSHIP:
First paragraph, p. 66, followed by paragraph beginning
"Change is the beginning," p. 68, *Belief in Human Life*.

PROCESSIONAL:
"We Gather Together," *People's Mass Book*, #53.

GREETING:
Christ has died, Christ is risen, Christ is with us still.
May the peace of the risen Christ be yours forever.

PRAYER OF INVOCATION:
By our prayer this day, Lord God,
   we proclaim the death of the Lord Jesus
   until he comes again.
For those who have faith in you,
   life merely changes, it never ceases.
We bring before you the memory of your servant (*name*)—
   all that is left to us.
You blessed us by her presence
   and now you are glorified by her faith.
In Jesus' name we pray,
   now and forever and ever.

FIRST READING:
1 Peter 1:3–12, followed by a period of reflection.

RESPONSE:
"Without Seeing You," *People's Mass Book*, #173.

THE GOSPEL:
John 14:8–19.

HOMILY

GENERAL INTENTIONS

PERIOD OF REFLECTION:
Intermission

PRAYER OF BLESSING OVER GIFTS:
"Pray, brothers, that my gift and yours . . ."

THE TABLE PRAYER

PREFACE:
Preface from Funeral Liturgy 1, this volume.

HYMN OF PRAISE:
"Holy God, We Praise Thy Name," *People's Mass Book,* #176.

ACCLAMATION AT CONSECRATION:
"Dying, you destroyed our death . . ."

ENDING ACCLAMATION:
"Keep in Mind," *People's Mass Book,* #145.

THE SERVICE OF COMMUNION

THE "OUR FATHER"

RITE OF PEACE

SONG:
"Psalm 162," *People's Mass Book,* #153.

PERIOD OF REFLECTION:
Intermission

THE DISMISSAL RITE

PRAYER OF BENEDICTION, BLESSING, AND DISMISSAL:
From the Funeral Liturgy, *The English-Latin Sacramentary.*

RECESSIONAL:
"To Paradise Now" in English translation.

AT THE CEMETERY
All from *The Experimental Liturgy Book,* pp. 158–159,
except final prayer which is read by all as follows: "We pray
that nothing" through "to be faithful to us in death," *Your Word
Is Near,* pp. 78–79.

HOMILY FOR FUNERAL LITURGY 2

*Note: The liturgy, and the homily which follows, was created
for the funeral of Dale Isham. He was a student and sixteen years
old when he was shot to death by an Oklahoma City police officer
on the evening of June 12, 1972. The policeman was exonerated
by the court on June 21, 1972. This homily was delivered at
Sacred Heart Church, June 22, 1972.*

Just a few weeks ago in every house of Christian worship the
usual Easter cry went up: "He is risen, He is not here!" The
statement itself appears without joy or rapture, and the fact is that
the first people to hear it ran away in fear and consternation and,
in their panic, they told no one anything about it. Their panic need
not surprise us, their consternation is all too understandable—
they are feelings we all share at this moment.

Looking at ———————— today you see nothing of that
word "Resurrection." And look at so many "living" people in the
world—the dullness, the dreary care, the endless routine, the
slavery, the violence, and the apparent desire to keep things exactly
the same. The fact that people say nothing new can happen, there
is no future, no one can come and deliver me, set me free—that
people openly yield to becoming stone, like tombs, is no wonder.
It's not surprising then that merchandise becomes more valuable
than life itself.

But for those of us who recall the Lord Jesus, his words ring
clear today. We place our values not on things that thieves and rust
can ruin; but rather life itself is our value. And while we cling to
this value against the attacks of those who would call us fools
and laugh at our apparent poverty and mock our freedom, we battle
a more serious enemy, a danger that springs from within. It is that
feeling of tiredness and confusion over the inadequacy of human
compassion, the lack of sense in the sufferings of our fellows,
the imperfection of human justice. Then too there are the less
seeable ruptures in the fabric of man—the pride and arrogance
holding sway in our homes, in our churches and in City Hall.

298

From all of these grows the real enemy that might destroy us—
it is the gnawing suspicion that our problems are insoluble, that we
are lost in a maze without exit, that the human race has at last
fallen flat on its face. If that enemy is gaining control of us, then
there isn't much left and we have no reason to hope.

But the fact is that, even so, hope is still born in the world, the
hope that there will be a hand that rescues us and sets us free,
someone who does what he says—and that this hope has not died;
that is the wonder!

We live in the shadow of catastrophe, yet we gather here in
hope and with some joy deep down. We pick up the broken
fragments of a boy's life and gather up the bits and pieces of our
own and we wonder over them; and we break bread remembering
another broken life—Jesus.

There are dreamers among us, men of vision and far-reaching
fantasy who write words like those we heard from the Book of
Revelation. Their news is that the final catastrophe for men has
already happened. It was a catastrophe of goodness, for the word of
God was flesh for us and his name was Jesus! In him is the city,
the dwelling place of man and of God.

All around us there is another city, full of pieces of desert.
Here many of us know the fear that everything—all our waiting for
fulfillment, for an answer—may just be an illusion. But there are
people in this city, and we must become people who go the way
of hope again and again; people who dare to build houses, love
each other; people who are full of cracks and holes, but who still do
not go under, who go on enduring this life, without hating and
without hitting back.

There are cities built everywhere from Atlanta to Berlin; and
people live in them, people who despite everything go on
recognizing their deepest dream in that Gospel about a young man
who was killed like the least of men and who was restored to honor
by his God. How we hope for that same restoration today.
Supported by the Gospel we have just heard, we trust that like the
dying wheat grain, this death is for us a new harvest time of hope;
that buried in this tragedy there is a new seed of life that makes
our city more human and more gentle.

We are all wishers, waiters-out-of wonder and hope. We gather in song and in silence to hear in new ways the Word of the vision and the dream of a day without tears. We gather to proclaim to each other and to hear again the good news that our deepest dream is history now. Jesus died and lives still, and where he is there too are his children. He unhides himself now in the bread and wine of this table and the flesh and blood of his people who approach.

All that we as his people can say is that we hope. We hope to be set free, we hope to be allowed to exist, we hope that someone will come for us, that rocks will change into springs and pools, and that there will be a city without death.

SELECTED SOURCES

PREFACES AND EUCHARISTIC PRAYERS

Discovery in Celebration, ed. Robert J. Heyer, Jack Podsiadlo, and Richard Payne (New York: Paulist Press, Copyright 1970 by The Missionary Society of St. Paul the Apostle in the State of New York).

The English-Latin Sacramentary for the United States of America, Catholic Book Publishing Co., New York, Copyright 1966 by Bishops' Commission on the Liturgical Apostolate; English translation of orations, prefaces, and similar material, Copyright 1957, 1961, 1966 by P. J. Kenedy & Sons.

Eucharistic Liturgies, ed. John Gallen, S.J. (New York: Newman Press, Copyright 1969 by The Missionary Society of St. Paul the Apostle in the State of New York).

The Experimental Liturgy Book, ed. Robert F. Hoey (New York: Herder and Herder, 1969).

Open Your Hearts, Huub Oosterhuis (New York: Herder and Herder, 1971).

The Underground Mass Book, ed. Stephen J. McNierney (Baltimore: Helicon, Copyright 1968 by Stephen J. McNierney).

STATEMENTS OF BELIEF

The Experimental Liturgy Book, ed. Robert F. Hoey (New York: Herder and Herder, 1969).

The Underground Mass Book, ed. Stephen J. McNierney (Baltimore: Helicon, Copyright 1968 by Stephen J. McNierney).

PRAYERS (INVOCATION, OFFERTORY, BENEDICTION)

Eucharistic Liturgies, ed. John Gallen, S.J. (New York: Newman Press, Copyright 1969 by The Missionary Society of St. Paul the Apostle in the State of New York).

Interrobang, Norman C. Habel (Philadelphia: Fortress Press, 1969).

Your Word Is Near, Huub Oosterhuis (New York: Newman Press, Copyright 1968 by The Missionary Society of St. Paul the Apostle in the State of New York).

GENERAL INTENTIONS

Your Word Is Near, Huub Oosterhuis (New York: Newman Press, Copyright 1968 by The Missionary Society of St. Paul the Apostle in the State of New York).

WEDDINGS, BAPTISMS, SPECIAL OCCASIONS

Home Celebrations, Lawrence E. Moser (New York: Newman Press, Copyright 1970 by The Missionary Society of St. Paul the Apostle in the State of New York).

Manual of Celebration, Robert Hovda (Washington, D.C.: The Liturgical Conference, Copyright 1969 by the International Committee on English in the Liturgy, Inc.).

READINGS, RESPONSES, INVITATIONS TO WORSHIP

The Jerusalem Bible, ed. Alexander Jones (New York: Doubleday & Co., Inc., 1966).

Lectionary for Mass (English Translation Approved by the National Conference of Catholic Bishops and Confirmed by the Apostolic See), *The Roman Missal* (Revised by Decree of the Second Vatican Council and Published by Authority of Pope Paul VI) (New York: Catholic Book Publishing Co., Copyright 1970 by the Confraternity of Christian Doctrine; International Copyright under International Copyright Union; all rights reserved under Pan-American Copyright Convention/English translation of the Introduction, Titles, Summaries and Antiphons Copyright 1969, International Committee on English in the Liturgy, Inc. All rights reserved).

Belief in Human Life, Anthony T. Padovano (New York: Paulist Press, Copyright 1969 by The Missionary Society of St. Paul the Apostle in the State of New York).

Children's Liturgies, ed. Virginia Sloyan and Gabe Huck (Washington, D.C.: The Liturgical Conference, 1970).

The Constitution on the Church, ed. Edward H. Peters (Glen Rock, N.J.: Deus Books, Paulist Press, Copyright 1965 by The Missionary Society of St. Paul the Apostle in the State of New York).

The Cost of Discipleship, Dietrich Bonhoeffer (New York: The Macmillan Co., 1963).

Discovery in Prayer, ed. Robert Heyer and Richard Payne (New York: Paulist Press, Copyright 1969 by The Missionary Society of St. Paul the Apostle in the State of New York).

Discovery in Song, ed. Robert Heyer (New York: Paulist Press, Copyright 1970 by The Missionary Society of St. Paul the Apostle in the State of New York).

Discovery in Word, ed. Robert J. Heyer (New York: Paulist Press, Copyright 1968 by The Missionary Society of St. Paul the Apostle in the State of New York).

The Documents of Vatican II, ed. Walter Abbott (New York: The America Press, 1966).

The Fables of Aesop, retold by Joseph Jacobs, reprinted by permission of The Macmillan Co. in *Coping,* Macmillan Gateway English Program, ed. Marjorie B. Smiley, *et al.* (New York: The Macmillan Co., 1966).

Faces of Freedom, ed. Adrianne Blue and Louis Savary (Winona, Minn.: St. Mary's College Press, 1969).

Free to Live, Free to Die, Malcolm Boyd (New York: Holt, Rinehart and Winston, Copyright 1967 by Malcolm Boyd).

God Speaks, Charles Peguy (New York: Pantheon Books, Inc., 1945).

He Is the Still Point of the Turning World, Mark Link, (Chicago: Argus Communications, 1971).

I've Got a Name, Holt's Impact Series, ed. Charlotte Brooks and Lawana Trout (New York: Holt, Rinehart & Winston, Inc., 1968).

Horizons of Hope, ed. Adrianne Blue and Louis Savary (Winona, Minn.: St. Mary's College Press, 1969).

Hymn of the Universe, Teilhard de Chardin, (New York: Harper & Row, Inc., 1965).

Journal of a Soul, Pope John XXIII (New York: McGraw-Hill Book Co., Copyright 1965 by Geoffrey Chapman, Ltd.).

304 *Selected Sources*

Listen to Love, ed. Louis M. Savary (New York: Regina Press, 1969).

The Little Prince, Antoine de Saint-Exupery (New York: Harcourt, Brace & World, 1943).

The Living Shakespeare, ed. O. J. Campbell (New York: The Macmillan Co., 1949).

My Life with Martin Luther King, Jr., Coretta Scott King (New York: Holt, Rinehart & Winston, 1969).

The New St. Andrew Bible Missal (New York: Benziger Brothers, Copyright 1966 by the Abbaye de St. Andre, Bruges, Belgium).

A New Catechism (New York: Herder and Herder, 1967).

95 Poems, e. e. cummings (New York: Harcourt, Brace & World, 1958).

Prayers, Michel Quoist (New York: Sheed & Ward, 1963).

Prayers for Pagans, Roger Bush (Dayton: Pflaum Press, 1969).

Prayers, Poems & Songs, Huub Oosterhuis (New York: Herder and Herder, 1970).

The Prophet, Kahlil Gibran (New York: Alfred A. Knopf, Renewal Copyright 1951 by Administrators C. T. A. of Kahlil Gibran Estate, & Mary G. Gibran).

Ritual and Life, ed. Maureen P. Collins, *et al.* (Winona, Minn.: St. Mary's College Press, 1970).

The Secular City, Harvey Cox (New York: The Macmillan Co., 1965).

Shaping of a Self, ed. Louis M. Savary, Jane C. Carter, and Charles Burke (Winona, Minn.: St. Mary's College Press, 1970).

The Sins of the Just, John H. McGoey (Milwaukee: Bruce Publishing Co., 1963).

Tender of Wishes, James Carroll (New York: Newman Press, Copyright 1969 by The Missionary Society of St. Paul the Apostle in the State of New York).

The Third Peacock, Robert Farrar Capon (Garden City, N.Y.: Doubleday & Co., 1971).

To Be Alive!, Alastair Reid (New York: The Macmillan Co., 1966).

To Kill a Mockingbird, Harper Lee (New York: J. P. Lippincott Co., Copyright 1960 by Harper Lee).

That Man Is You, Louis Evely (New York: Newman Press, Copyright 1964 by The Missionary Society of St. Paul the Apostle in the State of New York).

A Tree Grows In Brooklyn, Betty Smith (New York: Harper & Row Publishers, Inc., Copyright 1947 by Betty Smith).

The Underground Mass Book, ed. Stephen W. McNierney (Baltimore: Helicon, Copyright 1968 by Stephen W. McNierney).

The Unexpected Universe, Loren Eiseley (New York: Harcourt, Brace & World, Copyright 1969 by Loren Eiseley).

The Velveteen Rabbit, Margery Williams (Garden City, N.Y.: Doubleday, 1922).

Whitman, ed. Leslie A. Fiedler (New York: Dell Publishing Co., Inc., Copyright 1959 by Richard Wilbur).

MAGAZINES:

Critic
The Christian Herald
Ladies Home Journal
Life
Look
Sign
Voices: The Art and Science of Psychotherapy

MUSIC

Biblical Hymns and Psalms (Cincinnati: World Library of Sacred Music, 1965).

Biblical Hymns and Psalms, Vol. II (Cincinnati: World Library of Sacred Music, 1970).

Come Alive, Ray Repp (Chicago: F. E. L. Church Publications, Ltd., 1967).

The Hymnal of the Protestant Episcopal Church in the United States of America (New York: The Church Pension Fund, 1940).

Hymnal for Young Christians (Chicago: F. E. L. Church Publications, Ltd. 1967), Complete edition.

Hymnal for Young Christians, Vol. II (Chicago: F. E. L. Church Publications, Ltd. 1969).

Hymns for Now I (St. Louis: Walther League, 1967).

Our Parish Prays and Sings (Collegeville, Minn.: The Liturgical Press, Copyright 1959 by the Order of St. Benedict, Inc.).

People's Mass Book (Cincinnati: World Library of Sacred Music, 1970).

Psalms for Singing, Book One, S. Somerville (Cincinnati: World Library of Sacred Music, 1960).

Thirty Songs and Two Canticles (Toledo: Gregorian Institute of America, Copyright 1957 by The Grail, England).

Twenty-Four Psalms and a Canticle, Joseph Gelineau (Toledo: Gregorian Institute of America, Copyright 1955 by The Grail, England).

Yes, The Spirit Is A-Movin', Carey Landry (Washington, D.C.: Theological College Publications, 1969).

Hand in Hand, Joseph Wise (Cincinnati: World Library of Sacred Music, 1968).

INDEX OF THEMES, FESTIVALS, AND SPECIAL OCCASIONS